D0112711

Meet the New National Palace Museum

Preface of Recommendation

Opening a Door to Innovation

Since 1965, when the first opening its doors at the then new home in Wai-shuang-hsi on the outskirts of Taipei, the National Palace Museum (NPM) has undergone five phases of renovation and expansion. With the completion of the most recent one in February of 2007, the NPM now has a brand new look, both inside and out, for all to appreciate. We now provide a more ideal visiting environment and, by offering updated and more diverse educational activities, hopefully allow each and every visitor to the NPM experience the depth and variety of its collection.

In addition, through the application of digital technology, the publication of books and periodicals, and the production of derived merchandise, the value of NPM objects even more so knows no bounds of time or space. This guidebook "Meet the New National Palace Museum", which is published by Acoustiguide Asia (Taiwan Branch), provides introductions to the historical background and cultural development from the Neolithic age in remote antiquity to the late Ch'ing dynasty in the twentieth century. Complemented by in-depth and easy-to-read explanations, both general audiences and students of Chinese art alike will find more to appreciate and understand. Although there is no way to display the entire collection in its entirety all at once, this book plays the role of a fine yet concrete way of viewing the large from the small. It is greatly hoped that this book can serve as an unlimited extension of the NPM experience for all.

We firmly believe that the collection of the NPM, extending back for more than a thousand years, can still move and touch the hearts of modern people in the 21st century. In the future, we will continue to pursue modernizing and rejuvenation efforts for the NPM by engaging in the language of youth and modern thinking, spreading the spirit of the NPM even further. The cultural significance represented by the NPM is an unlimited source and the essence for its innovation. The NPM is an unparalleled trove of knowledge and cultural treasures, and I hope that both domestic and international friends will be able to enter even deeper realms of Chinese art and culture that lie herein with the help of this book.

Director, National Palace Museum

Kungshin Chou

Contents

Shedding Light on History   100

Corridors of Time

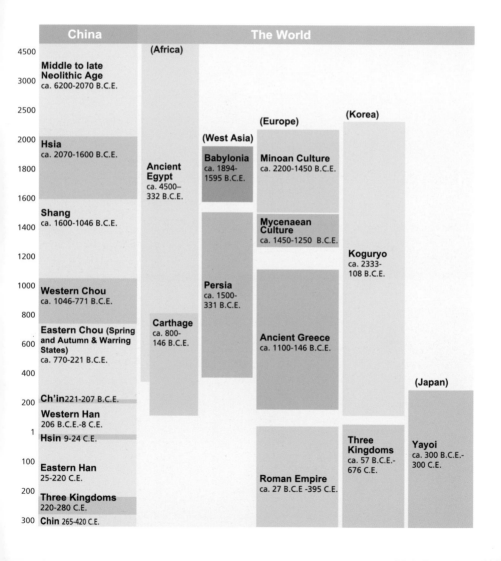

	China		The World			
4500		(Africa)				
3000	Middle to late Neolithic Age ca. 6200-2070 B.C.E.					
2500					(Europe)	(Korea)
2000	Hsia ca. 2070-1600 B.C.E.		(West Asia)			
1800		Ancient Egypt ca. 4500–332 B.C.E.	Babylonia ca. 1894-1595 B.C.E.	Minoan Culture ca. 2200-1450 B.C.E.		
1600	Shang ca. 1600-1046 B.C.E.					
1400				Mycenaean Culture ca. 1450-1250 B.C.E.		
1200					Koguryo ca. 2333-108 B.C.E.	
1000	Western Chou ca. 1046-771 B.C.E.		Persia ca. 1500-331 B.C.E.			
800		Carthage ca. 800-146 B.C.E.				
600	Eastern Chou (Spring and Autumn & Warring States) ca. 770-221 B.C.E.			Ancient Greece ca. 1100-146 B.C.E.		
400						(Japan)
200	Ch'in 221-207 B.C.E.					
	Western Han 206 B.C.E.-8 C.E.					Yayoi ca. 300 B.C.E.-300 C.E.
1	Hsin 9-24 C.E.				Three Kingdoms ca. 57 B.C.E.-676 C.E.	
100	Eastern Han 25-220 C.E.			Roman Empire ca. 27 B.C.E -395 C.E.		
200	Three Kingdoms 220-280 C.E.					
300	Chin 265-420 C.E.					

China	The World	(Korea)	(Japan)
		300	
Chin 265-420 C.E.	Roman Empire ca. 27 B.C.E. -395 C.E.		
	Western Roman Empire 395-476 C.E.	Three Kingdoms ca. 57 B.C.E.-676 C.E.	Kofun 300-592 C.E.
Northern & Southern Dynasties 316-589 C.E.			
Sui 581-618 C.E.			
			Asuka 592-709 C.E.
T'ang 618-907 C.E.	Byzantine Empire 395-1453 C.E.	Unified Silla 676-935 C.E.	
			Nara 710-793 C.E.
Five Dynasties & Ten Kingdoms 907-960 C.E.		Koryo 918-1392 C.E.	Heian 794-1192 C.E.
Northern Sung 960-1126 C.E.			
	Holy Roman Empire 962-1806 C.E.		
Southern Sung 1127-1279 C.E.			
			Kamakura 1192-1336 C.E.
Yüan 1271 -1368 C.E.			
			Nambokucho 1336-1392 C.E.
Ming 1368-1644 C.E.		Choson 1392-1910 C.E.	Muromachi 1392- 1573 C.E.
			Momoyama 1573-1603 C.E.
			Edo 1603-1868 C.E.
Ch'ing 1644-1911 C.E.			
			Meiji 1867-1911 C.E.

Year markers (left column): 300, 400, 500, 600, 700, 800, 900, 1000, 1100, 1200, 1300, 1400, 1500, 1600, 1700, 1800, 1900

The NPM over the Years

"There's a museum here in the hills. This island was originally just supposed to be a temporary passage for it. Now fate has brought it to stay."

—the film *The Passage*

Portrait of Emperor T'ai-tsung, T'ang dynasty

Portrait of Emperor Hui-tsung, Sung dynasty

Portrait of Emperor Shih-tsu (Kublai Khan), Yüan dynasty

The Emperors' Treasures

On 5 November 1924, the last emperor of China, P'u-i, was finally evicted from the Forbidden City, even though the Republic of China had already been established for more than a decade. Divestment of his symbolic status marked an end to the last vestiges of the then-defunct Ch'ing dynasty. The treasures in the Forbidden City and various palaces formed collections that had been amassed over the centuries and could be traced back through the courts of various dynasties. In many respects, they represented the essence of Chinese culture. In order to inventory these massive holdings and make preparations to establish a museum, the Republican government established the "Committee for the Disposition of Ch'ing Imperial Possessions." After more than nine months of organization and effort, the Palace Museum was officially inaugurated on National Day in 1925, October 10. An imperial collection of Chinese art and culture that had once been the private privilege of emperors had finally become a public heritage for the world to appreciate.

Portrait of Emperor Shih-tsung (Chia-ching), Ming dynasty

Portrait of Emperor Kao-tsung (Ch'ien-lung), Ch'ing dynasty

❶ 1933　Peking →Shanghai

❷ 1936　Shanghai →Nanking

❸ 1937　Nanking →O-mei

　　　　　Nanking →Lo-shan

　　　　　Nanking →Pa-hsien

❹ 1946　O-mei →Chungking

　　　　　Lo-shan →Chungking

　　　　　Pa-hsien →Chungking

❺ 1947　Chungking →Nanking

❻ 1948　Nanking →Taiwan

Suffering and Wandering

Even after the museum opened, however, inventory work continued. In addition to holding exhibitions, the publication of books and periodicals also began. As many know, the first half of the twentieth century was a period of great turmoil and transition in China, which ultimately had an enormous influence on the fate of the museum and its collection. The Mukden Incident on 18 September 1931, instigated by Japanese troops occupying Manchuria to the north, led to increasing tension. To safeguard the museum collection from potential harm due to armed conflict, the government began the task of removing the objects in crates to Shanghai in February of 1933. Temporarily held in warehouses in the foreign concessions, they were later transported to newly constructed storage facilities in Nanking. After full-scale war erupted between China and Japan in 1937, the objects were then moved in three shipments westward to O-mei, Lo-shan, and Pa-hsien. Not until 1946, after the end of World War II, was the scattered collection reunited again in Nanking. Though the objects went unscathed during this tumultuous journey, it did not represent the end of the story. In the ensuing chaos of civil war that broke out between the Nationalists of the Republican government and the Communists, it was decided to move some of the best of the collection across the Taiwan Strait at the end of 1948 for safekeeping in Taiwan. This portion of the collection thus came to set foot on the island of Taiwan in the form of the National Palace Museum.

A World-class Museum

After the artworks and cultural objects arrived in Taiwan, they were first transported and stored at Pei-kou in Wu-feng Village, Taichung County. In addition to many masterpieces from the Palace Museum, there were objects from the collections of other mainland institutions, such as the Central Library, the Institute of History and Philology of Academia Sinica, and the Preparatory Office of the Central Museum. Later the government decided to construct a new home for the collection in the Taipei suburb of Wai-shuang-hsi, which was completed and opened to the public in 1965. Since moving to Taipei, the facilities of the National Palace Museum have undergone several expansion projects for exhibition and storage space. In other museum endeavors, such as research, publishing, and international exchange, considerable advances have also been made. The National Palace Museum of today not only holds a world-class collection of objects, it is also up to date with the latest international museum standards in every regard.

Unlocking the NPM Codes

While browsing through the National Palace Museum, have you noticed the contents of the labels for each object on display?

These labels or explanatory texts include not only the name of the object, but also relevant information on the period it was made or person who made it. Many labels have a serial number known as an accession number. The first part of this code is composed of two Chinese characters, the first identifying the source and the latter the type of object.

The majority of objects in the National Palace Museum come from the former Peking Palace Museum collection and the Preparatory Office of the Nanking Central Museum. The Peking Palace Museum took charge of the court collection in the Forbidden City, while the Preparatory Office of the Nanking Central Museum was established in 1933, mainly to take over management of the collections from various Ch'ing palaces. The part of these holdings moved to Taiwan included more than 600,000 objects. Afterwards, additions in the form of purchases, donations, and entrustments have resulted in the collection already exceeding 650,000 (as of 2006).

Different sources for the objects led to the use of varying initial characters in the accession numbers. The characters for *ku* 故, *chung* 中, *tseng* 贈, and *kou* 購, for example, stand for the following four sources, respectively: the Peking Palace Museum, the Preparatory Office of the Nanking Central Museum, donations, and purchases. The second character in the accession number represents the type of object. *Shu* 書, for instance, stands for calligraphy, *t'ung* 銅 for bronze, *shan* 善 for rare book, *tien* 殿 for imprint by the Wu-ying Palace in the Forbidden City, *wen* 文 for studio object, *fo* 佛 for Buddhist scripture, and so on.

These accession numbers, though appearing inconspicuous, actually contain a wealth of information about the objects, offering important information in collection management and for researchers.

北宋
汝窯　青瓷花式溫碗

Warming bowl in the shape of a flower with light greenish-blue glaze

Porcelain, Ju ware
Northem Sung dynasty, early 12th century

故瓷16929/呂一九一二

戰國中期
嵌綠松石金屬絲犧尊

Cow-shaped *tsun* with turquoise and metallic thread inlays

Middle Warring States Period
ca. 5th to 3rd century B.C.E

呂三七四/故銅2382

明　永樂
穿蓮龍紋天球瓶

Celestial globe vase with underglaze blue decoration of dragon among lotus blossoms

Ming dynasty, Yung-lo reign (1403-1424)

闕四三七/故瓷12547/院1738箱

N

To Shilin

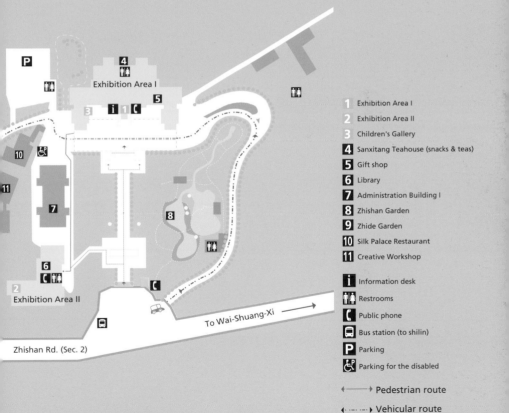

P Parking

🚻 Restrooms

4 🚻
Exhibition Area I

🚻

3 **i** **C**

5

10

♿🅿

11

7

8

🚻

6
C 🚻

2
Exhibition Area II

C

🚌

To Wai-Shuang-Xi ⟶

Zhishan Rd. (Sec. 2)

1 Exhibition Area I

2 Exhibition Area II

3 Children's Gallery

4 Sanxitang Teahouse (snacks & teas)

5 Gift shop

6 Library

7 Administration Building I

8 Zhishan Garden

9 Zhide Garden

10 Silk Palace Restaurant

11 Creative Workshop

i Information desk

🚻 Restrooms

C Public phone

🚌 Bus station (to shilin)

P Parking

♿🅿 Parking for the disabled

◄———► Pedestrian route

◄·—·—·► Vehicular route

Spirits of the Heavens and Earth

The Neolithic Age

The Bronze Age

The Ch'in and Han Dynasties

Dazzling Gems of the Palaces

The Neolithic Age (6200-1600 B.C.E.)

The Yellow and Yangtze River valleys are the cradles of ancient Chinese civilization. More than 8,000 years ago, inhabitants in various parts of what is now Mainland China had already entered the middle Neolithic Age. Settling down as they raised livestock and farmed the land in tribal life helped support advances in other pursuits, such as refining techniques for grinding stone and making pottery. They fired increasingly refined pottery and developed methods for carving jade. As jade (in particular the nephrite variety) became appreciated for its beauty, toughness, and warm luster, people came to believe that this mineral possessed special "powers" that could be called its "spirit." For this reason, jade was not only ground into beautiful objects for decoration but also as ritual objects for ceremonies dedicated to the spirits of the heavens and earth.

Designs and forms of jades, along with symbols engraved on them, also reveal the spiritual side of people's beliefs. In the northeast along the coast, for example, emerged the legend of the "dark bird," which led to the creation of numerous jades related to birds. Peoples of the western highlands, on the other hand, tended to favor simple jade objects either undecorated or bearing geometric designs.

The late Neolithic Age thus represented the dawn of Chinese civilization. The ideals of "revering jade" and "appreciating jade" apparently formulated then continued down to the present day, forming one of the hallmarks of Chinese culture through the millennia.

The Northeastern Region
The Lower Yellow River Valley
Western China Proper
The Lower Yangtze River Valley

The Northeastern Region

Seven to eight thousand years ago, the Hsing-lung-wa Culture emerged in the area north of modern-day Yen-shan in the Liao-ning area west of the Liao River. Its peoples had already learned to carve fine jade into small tools and decorative objects.

In the Hung-shan Culture of five to six thousand years ago that emerged there, it was perhaps because people believed that the mystery of life had been transmitted to their ancestors from the gods in the form of a "dark bird" (that is, a bird of prey in flight) that they carved many jades on the subject of birds of prey. In addition, they also created images of various other animals, such as bears, tigers, and pigs. As evidence of the magical spirit of life, these peoples also went so far as to combine the parts of various animals, birds, and human figures in single objects. Perhaps those who made and used these items sought to communicate with the gods and their ancestors through the magic of jade and the spirits of animals, thereby offering prayers for peace and well-being.

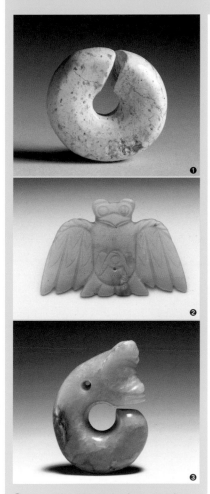

❶Jade *chüeh* earring, Hsing-lung-wa Culture
People in the Hsing-lung-wa Culture ground beautiful pieces of jade to make round ear ornaments such as this.

❷Jade bird pendant, Hung-shan Culture

❸Jade "pig-dragon," Hung-shan Culture

Hooked cloud-shaped pendant, Hung-shan Culture
The outer forms of this cloud-shaped jade ornament also look like curved talons or bird beaks and thus perhaps related to belief in the "dark bird" of the Hung-shan Culture.

The Lower Yellow River Valley

Ancient documents mostly refer to the inhabitants of the lower Yellow River valley in the Shantung region as belonging to the "Eastern Yi tribes." Archaeological evidence indicates that people of the Ta-wen-k'ou Culture, who lived five to six thousand years ago, had by later stages already developed techniques for firing tough, high-temperature white and black forms of pottery.

Appearing more than 4,000 years ago, the Shantung type of the Lung-shan Culture also developed in this region. Noted for its advanced techniques of black pottery production, these wares not only have walls as thin as egg shells but are also solid enough to do openwork. The jade carvings of these peoples were also exceptionally elegant. The totemic spirit-ancestor figures they produced, for example, combine the large whorl-eyes of figures from the northeast in the Yen and Liao areas with the arrow-shaped *chieh* 介 character treasure-crown forms from the lower reaches of the Yangtze River in the Kiangnan region and the flowing spiral pattern of hooked lines.

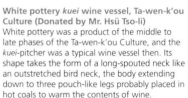

White pottery *kuei* wine vessel, Ta-wen-k'ou Culture (Donated by Mr. Hsü Tso-li)

White pottery was a product of the middle to late phases of the Ta-wen-k'ou Culture, and the *kuei*-pitcher was a typical wine vessel then. Its shape takes the form of a long-spouted neck like an outstretched bird neck, the body extending down to three pouch-like legs probably placed in hot coals to warm the contents of wine.

Jade *kuei*-tablet, Shantung Lung-shan Culture

This form of bladed jade instrument was used in ancient ceremonies to symbolize the ruler's status, and in statutes of rituals it was referred to as a *kuei*. The middle portion of this jade *kuei*-tablet is engraved with a spirit-ancestor decoration in low relief, which probably was the source of the "animal-mask pattern" found on various objects later in the Bronze Age.

Jade carving had already appeared six to seven thousand years ago in the Kiangnan region of the lower Yangtze River valley, and by four to five thousand years ago, the Liang-chu Culture there had reached a peak of development. An axe-head form carved in jade, known as a *yüeh*, became a shaman's symbol of authority by holding this instrument in ceremonies. The shaman may have also used the round jade *pi*-disc and square *ts'ung*-tube with its inner round hole to communicate between the heavens and earth. These peoples also revered a similar "dark bird," which is engraved on some jade discs as a symbol for the "bird standing on an altar" to communicate with the heavens. The jade *ts'ung* tube was also often carved with a mask pattern splayed right and left from each corner, bearing small and large eyes.

Western China Proper

The traditional western regions of China proper consist of the middle and upper reaches of the Yellow River as it surges through the thick, loess plateaus there. The inhabitants of this area some four to seven thousand years ago excelled at producing colored pottery and also painted abstract water and continuous patterns on their fired clay pots. The jades they made were mainly ritual objects and mostly simple, geometric forms. Large numbers of round *pi*-discs and square *ts'ung*-tubes found there may have been used to reflect the ancient Chinese

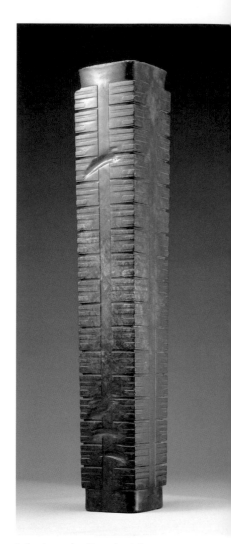

Jade *ts'ung*-tube, Liang-chu Culture
Tall, segmented *ts'ung*-tubes made of jade such as this became quite popular in the late phase of the Liang-chu Culture.

belief of the universe as comprised of a round heavens and a square earth.

The legendary common ruler of the western regions known as the "Yellow Emperor" (Huang-ti) is said to have later led his tribes in victory over the Eastern Yi peoples to the east. As a result, this area became the political center of several dynasties thereafter, such as the Hsia and Chou, and a fountainhead for many features of ancient Chinese civilization that were to emerge there. For example, numerous bladed jades have been excavated in this region, perhaps testifying to records in later Han dynasty books of the "period of the Yellow Emperor, who used jades as weapons."

Colored pottery jar, Ma-chia-yao Culture (Ma-ch'ang phase)
This orange-reddish pot was one of the most common pottery types of the Ma-chia-yao Culture. The decoration features seven round forms around the middle that perhaps reflect the continuity of life and a pursuit of eternity that formed part of the thought of prehistoric inhabitants in the western part of China proper.

Jade *pi*-disc, Lung-shan/Ch'i-chia Culture system
The western regions of Mainland China are a rich source of raw jade that allowed the production of magnificent large-scale ritual objects.

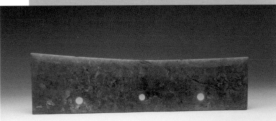

Jade knife, Lung-shan/Ch'i-chia Culture system

The Bronze Age (1600-221 B.C.E.)

Ancient Chinese civilization expanded roughly around the time of the Shang and Chou dynasties, which corresponded to the era of magnificent productions in bronze.

The casting of bronzes requires great skill, a command of vast human and mineral resources, and a strict division of labor, so only those with great power and materials —strong rulers—could have made and owned them. Bronzes thus came to symbolize their status. Rulers actively promoted the craft of bronzes, as a stream of innovations in form and decoration poured forth to serve as a concrete display of culture and authority.

This was also a period in which the production of jade, stone, ivory, bone, and pottery objects also flourished. The status of jade at this time was second only to bronze, as both of these materials came to represent the highest achievements in material culture and technology.

The Shang to Early Western Chou

The establishment of a system of ritual statutes and music became an important standard for maintaining state order in ancient China. In the early Shang dynasty, for instance, sets of bronze wine vessels comprised of the *ku, chüeh, chia, ho, lei, tsun,* and *yu* were complemented by those for food consisting of the *ting, li,* and *kuei.* Water vessel sets including the *yü* and *p'an* appeared in later periods. Bronze vessels served as the most important ritual implements in this period. As for jades, the Neolithic Age ritual traditions behind such instruments as the *pi*-disc, *ts'ung*-tube, *kuei*-tablet, and *chang*-tablet continued, as these increasingly became auspicious objects symbolizing the status of the person leading a ceremony.

Chu-ke-fu-ting *ho*, early Western Chou dynasty

The animal-mask, phoenix-bird, and *k'uei*-dragon often seen in decoration on bronzes and jades of this era served as media for communication between the heavens and ancestral spirits during ceremonies. These mysterious, awe-inspiring forms reflected people's reverence of nature and the spirit world. Some nobility also had their clan insignias cast on bronzes they had made, identifying and demonstrating their authority and meritorious achievement. They thus hoped to communicate the pride and joy of the clan by revering their ancestors.

Bronze was not only cast into ritual objects, but also into hard, sharp weapons. A ruler who could furnish his armies with bronze weapons had a distinct advantage over others, so bronze technology became an important key to solidifying power and expanding one's realm.

Ya-ch'ou square *kuei*, late Shang dynasty
The Ya-ch'ou clan active in the Shantung area during the late Shang dynasty sponsored the production of more-difficult-to-make square-shaped bronzes. The handles of this square-*kuei* vessel, for example, are designed as three-dimensional shapes in the form of lively animal heads biting onto the bodies of small birds. This type of dramatic expression became a distinctive characteristic of bronzes made by the Ya-ch'ou clan.

Nao bells with animal-mask designs, late Shang dynasty
The *nao*-bell was an important bronze percussion musical instrument in the Shang dynasty.

Yüeh axe inlaid with an animal mask in turquoise, late Shang dynasty
The *yüeh*, a weapon similar in function to an axe, later became a symbol of political and military rule. This exquisite *yüeh* inlaid with turquoise must have been an important ritual object.

The Western Chou

Bronzes of the early Western Chou dynasty mainly followed the style of splendor exhibited in the late Shang dynasty. Middle and late Chou bronzes, on the other hand, reveal many innovations in forms, such as the *fu, hsü,* and *p'u* food vessels. Bells made and used as sets, as well as *p'an* and *yi* water basins, also witnessed considerable development. As for decoration, the phoenix-bird pattern became increasingly popular as the animal-mask pattern was transformed into such commonly found geometric designs of continuous loops and vertical scales. These forms of decoration were often designed to continue around the vessel for a harmonious effect that seems to reflect the pursuit of beauty and order in a society founded on ritual and music.

In addition to a variety of vessel shapes and decorations, the instances and number of characters cast or engraved on bronzes (known as "gold writing")

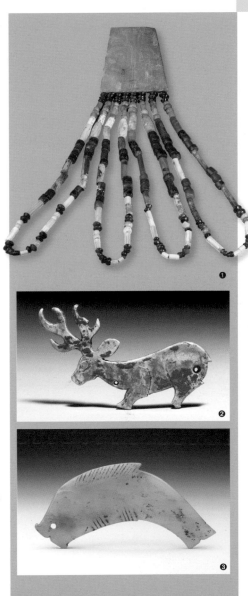

❶Trapezoid jade pendants, Western Chou dynasty
A plaque in the form of a trapezoid made mainly of jade or ivory, with suspended strings of jade, was popular in the Western Chou dynasty. This pendant with strings of beads was unearthed from the tomb of a female member of nobility, worn in an area corresponding to the person's right shoulder and suspended down to the waist.
❷Deer-shaped jade pendant, Western Chou dynasty
❸Fish-shaped jade pendant, Western Chou dynasty

rose dramatically. Not only did this form of writing play a decisive role in molding the foundations of Chinese calligraphy, it is also a precious first-hand source of historical information. Clan insignias had appeared on the late Shang bronzes along with short inscriptions. Later, the contents gradually expanded in length, from a short blessing such as "May descendants cherish this forever" from the reign of the Chou king K'ang to the lengthy inscriptions of more than a hundred characters in the middle and later Chou dynasty. Those who had bronzes made often used them to announce and display their achievements or merits, or to record an important event. Serving as an

important memento for eternity, and to pay respects to one's ancestors, they were used in ceremonies to honor ancestors and to be passed down in the family.

Jades were still revered at this time, even as the production of bronzes flourished. Not only did the nobility use and appreciate jades in their lifetime, jades continued to serve an important ritual purpose as funerary objects after death to be interred in tombs. Jades thereby demonstrated a person's wealth, status, and moral integrity in the afterworld as well. Nobility at the time often wore jade pendants assembled into sets as part of their status symbols, and

San *p'an*, late Western Chou dynasty
The inscription on the San *p'an*, cast on the inside of the vessel, records a contract between two states in the Western Chou period. The contents indicate that the State of Tse had encroached on the land of San, resulting in a dispute. Later the two states came to an agreement in which Tse would cede land as compensation for damages. The inscription consists of 357 characters done in solid yet beautiful lines, making this a masterpiece in the art of "bronze script" calligraphy.

Sung *hu*, late Western Chou dynasty

Mao-kung *ting*, late Western Chou dynasty
The 500 characters cast on the inside of this *ting* made in the reign of King Hsüan of Chou stand as the longest inscription of any bronze found so far. The contents describe how King Hsüan came to rely on Mao-kung (Duke Mao), who carried out the monarch's policies and was richly rewarded for doing so. That is why Duke Mao had this bronze *ting* cast, so as to pass it on to his descendants.

many pieces were carved into dragon-and-phoenix, human-face, and animal designs. Jades used in funerals took the form of symbols for parts of the face, creating a mask to cover the face of the dead. There were also jade fish and jade cicadas placed in the mouth of the deceased in the hopes that the magical qualities they were thought to possess would preserve the body intact after death.

Tsung-chou bell, late Western Chou dynasty
The Tsung-chou bell is a rare example of an object personally ordered by a Chou king. The inscription cast in 123 characters narrates how King Li of the Chou conquered the state of P'u, achieving great victory in the submission of 27 states in the south.

The Eastern Chou (Spring and Autumn & Warring States)

Into the Chou dynasty, the central authority of the king gradually diminished as regional vassals rose and sought domination. The system of rites and music also fragmented with this decline of Chou rule. Vassals, with their new power, sought to demonstrate their authority as they competed also in the field of crafts. This corresponded to the period of a "hundred schools" of philosophy contending with each other as well as a rise in trade and commerce. These factors, combined with interaction that took place with other peoples, gave rise to unprecedented plurality and innovation in the forms and decoration of bronzes, pottery, ivory carvings, jades, and other objects. It was also a time when greater attention was placed on practical functions in life.

Bronzes, with the emergence of the lost-wax method of casting, become much more refined and intricate in form and design. As for decoration, advances took place in inlay techniques as well as inlaid silver and gold. Complemented by popular patterns of coiling serpents and dragons, the art of bronzes thus entered into a golden age of splendor and refinement.

Peoples living on the outskirts of these regional states often had the opportunity to engage in exchange with Chinese civilization through a number of channels, and one result was distinctive bronze cultures with their own unique forms and designs. Such works have

A set of bells of Tzu-fan chime (8 pieces in total), middle Spring and Autumn period
The Tzu-fan set of harmonized bells includes a set of inscriptions that testify to certain aspects of the historical record, such as how Duke Wen of Chin recovered control of his state as well as the war between the states of Chin and Ch'u. The person who had this set made, Tzu-fan, was an uncle of Duke Wen.

become an important source of information for scholars of other ancient peoples on the margins of Chinese culture.

After Ch'in shih-huang, the first emperor of the Ch'in who unified China, established his empire in the late third century BCE, he implemented policies to establish a unified writing system, road width, and system of weights and measures. A large number of weights and measures, along with the edicts inscribed on them, testify to this historical fact. Thus, the era of classical Chinese civilization came to an end with the rise of the short-lived Ch'in empire, as China headed into a glorious age represented by the Western and Eastern Han periods, when important traditions of Chinese culture were founded.

Cow-shaped *tsun* with turquoise and metallic thread inlays, middle Warring States period
The art of inlay, with its origins in the Shang dynasty, involved at this time a combination of turquoise and various metals on a wide variety of vessel forms, bringing the art of bronze to another peak of development.

Tsun in the shape of a bird-headed animal, early Warring States period

Ting with stylized animal-mask pattern, Warring States period

Dagger with double-ringed pommel, late Spring and Autumn to middle Warring States period
The handle and pommel of this dagger feature a double-ring design, which is often found on weapons made in the north (Hopeh, Inner Mongolia, Ning-hsia, and the northeast).

The Ch'in and Han Dynasties

(221 B.C.E.-220 C.E.)

The short Ch'in dynasty and much longer Han dynasty was a time when the feudal system of the Shang and Chou dynasties was transformed into the political entity of an empire controlling the entire country. The Han policy of singling out Confucianism as the form of state thought laid the foundation for the supreme and long-lasting status it has enjoyed in Chinese history. In the lives of everyday people, much greater attention was also placed on practical needs, resulting in a rich variety of functional objects for daily use.

Many traditions that would have a key influence on later Chinese culture appeared in the Ch'in and Han period, making this era crucial to the transition from "classicism" to "tradition." Solid foundations in both material and spiritual culture of this time helped form the "Heyday of the Great Han," spurring the rise of the Han dynasty that rivaled the Roman Empire in the West.

Material Culture

People in the Ch'in and Han period were serious about the here and now, and this attitude is reflected in the rich and varied objects of everyday life. These include measures, vessels for food and drink, and wine containers, warmers, and cups related to the culture of wine prevalent at the time. It is also seen in lamps for providing light, water vessels, bronze mirrors for personal use, and jade pendants, seals, and daggers that a gentleman wore.

The majority of the Ch'in and Han dynasty objects in the National Palace Museum come from the former Ch'ing dynasty collection, and those on display here are mostly made of bronze and jade, though some are also rendered in ceramic. These particular objects would have been used by members of the upper classes, and some pieces of gray pottery might have been funerary items.

Bronze *hsiang-lou* wine vessel, Han dynasty

The majority of these objects of daily use could also be handed down to later generations, the style of these forms revealing the unique majesty and beauty of Han dynasty arts and crafts.

Jade horn-shaped drinking cup with dragon design, Han dynasty
The shape of this cup is similar to that of a rhinoceros horn, sporting the spirited body of a dragon carved on its surface. The craftsmanship is exquisite, reflecting a combination of the culture of reverence for the dragon in the Han dynasty and influences of the horn-cup shape from Western Asia.

Pottery *hu* in the shape of a cocoon, Han dynasty
This example of black wine pottery is in a shape resembling a silkworm cocoon, revealing a simple yet elegantly beautiful form. More than a thousand years later, the Ch'ien-lung Emperor in the Ch'ing dynasty appreciated the vessel so much as to have his poetry in praise of its beauty engraved on the surface.

Spiritual Culture

The Han dynasty was a time when people held special respect for the world of spirits and immortals. For this reason, forms, decoration, and inscriptions for many everyday objects and ritual implements were closely related to this notion.

Subject matter related to the dragon-phoenix pair, Four Spirit Animals (green dragon, white tiger, red bird, and black tortoise), clouds-and-mists decoration, patterns of the stars, mountains of the immortals, and human figures with wings became popular at this time, reflecting Han dynasty ideas about the universal order of things and yearnings for the realm of immortality. Likewise, such auspicious phrases as "Eternal happiness with no end," "Unbroken line of descendants," and "Long life everlasting" were also well-received, demonstrating the importance of the here and now in the Han dynasty.

Bronze *po-shan lu* incense burner, Han dynasty
The *po-shan* ("Po Mountain") censer was used to burn incense or perfume clothes. Smoke would rise through the openwork holes of these mountains of immortals. Suggesting radiant mists in a miniature landscape, it also created the illusion of a world of immortals that had been conjured and aspired to by people in the Han dynasty.

Jade *pi-hsieh* animal, Han dynasty
The *pi-hsieh* is a spirit beast of legend that means "evil averter." As the name suggests, people thought that it possessed supernatural power to repel evil influences and dispel demons. It was visualized in the form of a lion but also with wings. This combination, which appeared approximately in the Western Han dynasty, had been brought to China from Western Asia.

Bronze *chia* mirror, Han dynasty
For people of the Han dynasty, a mirror was not just a tool to check one's appearance, but it also had cultural significance with auspicious overtones for radiating light and repelling evil. For this reason, many bronze mirrors have been recovered from Han dynasty tombs, and the backs of these mirrors are often filled with decorative images of the spirit realm and auspicious phrases rendered in relief.

***Pi*-disc of everlasting happiness, Eastern Han dynasty**
This jade reveals certain features of Han dynasty spiritual culture. The outer rim is carved in openwork with images of the "green dragon," "white tiger," "red bird," and "black tortoise"--spirit animals representing the directions of east, west, south, and north, as well as the four seasons of spring, summer, autumn, and winter, respectively. The upper and lower borders along the central axis are carved with the auspicious character-combination of "everlasting" and "happiness" in openwork carving, respectively.

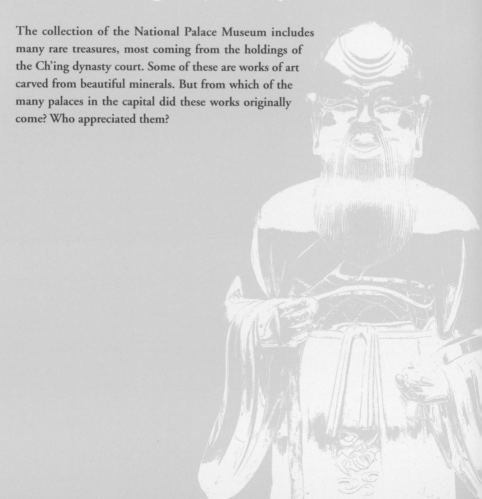

Dazzling Gems from the Ch'ing Dynasty Palaces

The collection of the National Palace Museum includes many rare treasures, most coming from the holdings of the Ch'ing dynasty court. Some of these are works of art carved from beautiful minerals. But from which of the many palaces in the capital did these works originally come? Who appreciated them?

Jadeite cabbage, Ch'ing dynasty
This jade sculpture was originally located in the Yung-ho Palace and might well have been part of the dowry of the Kuang-hsü Emperor's Consort Chin, who lived there. Jade craftsmen carved the white part of the jadeite to represent the brilliant white stalks, with the emerald green rendered at the top to represent the leafy parts. The end result is a beautifully lustrous and realistic head of bok choy. The white portion not only symbolizes the purity of the emperor's new bride, the addition of a katydid and locust (known for their propensity to multiply in great numbers) on the leaves at the top represents auspicious overtones to beget many children. Thus, this piece was probably meant as a gift blessing the bride with numerous children for the emperor.

White jade branch of elegant lychee, Ch'ing dynasty
This piece was from originally in the Ch'ien-ch'ing Palace.

The Yung-shou and Yung-ho Palaces

Flanking the eastern and western sides of the Forbidden City in Peking is an orderly arrangement of six palaces known as the "Six Palaces of the East" and "Six Palaces of the West." These were the residences of the empress and imperial consorts. Among them, the Yung-shou Palace was where the Shun-chih Emperor's favored concubine, Consort Tung-o, lived in the early Ch'ing. Later, the Yung-cheng Emperor had this palace converted into one of his resting places. The Yung-ho Palace was where Kuang-hsü's favorite Consort Chin lived in the late Ch'ing dynasty. The splendid objects that once adorned these palaces no doubt reflected the beauty of their owners.

The Ch'ien-ch'ing Palace

From the time the Ch'ien-ch'ing Palace was built in the Yung-lo reign in the Ming dynasty up until the reign of the K'ang-hsi Emperor in the Ch'ing dynasty, it served as the residential palace for sixteen emperors. Not only the place for everyday life of the emperor, it was also where he managed government affairs, convened with officials, and received visiting foreign envoys.

The Yang-hsin Hall

Starting with the Yung-cheng Emperor in the Ch'ing dynasty, the Yang-hsin Hall served as the residential palace of the emperor. Treasures stored there reflected the imperial taste of its occupant.

The Shou-huang Hall

The Shou-huang Hall was located on the artificial mountain in the northern part of the Forbidden City. Starting from the Ch'ien-lung reign, it was used as the place to enshrine and worship portraits and tapestry images of the Ch'ing imperial ancestors.

Jadeite screen insert, Ch'ing dynasty
This work and its stand were originally from the Shou-huang Hall.

Meat-shaped stone, Ch'ing dynasty
Originally stored in the Yang-hsin Hall, the natural features of this mineral have been adapted and accentuated in the form of delicate carving and dyeing to create a sculpture that looks incredibly like a piece of stewed pork. The artisans' detail and sense of naturalism displayed here are amazing.

The Rise of Civilization

The Six Dynasties to Sui and T'ang Period (221 - 960)

Ascending the stairs from the lobby to the right wing of the second floor of the National Palace Museum main building, the visitor is greeted by ceramic sculptures of a T'ang dynasty lady and *san-ts'ai* ("tricolor") official. Standing solemnly under the lights, they reflect the glory of history and cultural objects from this period. China in this era witnessed the end of more than 270 years of constant warfare. This period of troubled times had started with the disintegration of the Three Kingdoms and was followed by chaos in the War of the Eight Princes of the Western Chin, battles among the Sixteen Kingdoms of Five Ethnic Groups, and the retreat of the Eastern Chin to Kiangnan. Only later were the kingdoms that had sprung up at this time conquered one by one to create a single unity—the short–lived Sui dynasty, which was followed by the T'ang dynasty. Unification brought arts and crafts in China to another pinnacle, as the art forms of both neighboring steppes and foreign states came into China and formed a new fusion of domestic and foreign styles unlike what had ever been seen before.

Pottery

The type of pottery known as "T'ang *san-ts'ai*," the latter part translating as "tricolor," refers to a kind of low-temperature glazed-color pottery popular in the T'ang dynasty. Although the main colors are yellow, green, and white (hence the name), it actually can feature a wide variety of other hues, such as ochre-red, bright purple, or cobalt blue. The colors are applied using batik, splash, and sprinkle techniques to create an extremely free and fluid effect.

The popularity of tricolor wares was closely related to the sumptuous funerary practices of the High T'ang period, the unbridled colors and clever forms quickly developing to keep up with their demand as funerary objects for the upper classes. A wide array of funerary subjects, such as civil officials and generals, dancers and musicians, and even horses and camels (as well as various vessels) all became popular at this time.

Figurine of a standing lady with painted colors, Pottery, T'ang dynasty (Donated by Mr. Tsui Tsin-tong)
The lady's extremely delicate eyebrows and rounded plump face (along with her tall, elaborate hairstyle and large, flowing robes rendered with succinct yet descriptive lines) all highlight the manner and appearance of this age of prosperity.

Porcelain

"Greens of the south and whites of the north" was an expression used to describe the renown of southern China for its production of celadon wares and the north for its white wares during the Sui and T'ang dynasties.

More specifically, southern green wares referred to celadons fired in the Yüeh kilns, while northern whites were the white porcelains made at the Hsing kilns in Hopeh.

The firing of gray-bodied celadon porcelains in the south began in the Eastern Han dynasty. By the Six Dynasties period, celadons were being produced with lustrous, even glaze in elegant forms and incised patterns for decoration. The art of celadons matured in the T'ang dynasty, and the best porcelains of the Yüeh kilns were greatly appreciated and even sent to the court as tribute for imperial use. The pure, white-bodied wares with glistening and translucent white glaze fired at the Hsing and Ting kilns in the north became widely used among the populace. As Li Chao in the T'ang dynasty wrote in *Amendments to the History of the Dynasty*, "The white porcelain bowls of Nei-ch'iu and the purple stone ink slabs of Tuan-hsi are used throughout the land by rich and poor alike." Here, "Nei-ch'iu" (modern Nei-ch'iu, Hopeh) refers to the abundant production of white porcelains at the Hsing kilns there. The clay used to mold Hsing porcelains, with its low percentage of iron, resulted in its pure white color. This is why it won the praise of Lu Yu in his *Classic of Tea* for the beauty of its whiteness, which he compared to that of pure silver and snow.

❶

❶Vase with double dragon-shaped handles in white glaze, Porcelain, T'ang dynasty

The most outstanding feature of this double-dragon handled vase is the form of two dragons creating the handles. The mouths of the dragons bite onto the rim as if to take a drink from the contents. Complemented by the slender neck and wide, rounded form of the body, the overall shape of the vase is that of upright weightiness yet rich with a sense of flow and animation.

❷Basin in *mi-se* green glaze, Porcelain, Yüeh ware, Five Dynasties period

Tribute porcelains from Yüeh-chou used at the inner court were known starting from the middle of the T'ang dynasty as *mi-se*, or "secret color," perhaps due to the mysterious wormwood-leaf color of its glaze. In any case, the ability to control the exact amount of ferric oxide in the glaze and the firing time perfectly to yield this glaze was extremely difficult.

❸Vase with loops in white glaze, Porcelain, Hsing ware, T'ang dynasty

This porcelain vessel features a short neck and an oval body. A pair of corresponding loop handles are found at the bottom near the foot and on the shoulders, which would have allowed this vase to be fastened with a rope in a style reminiscent of that used on the steppes.

The Sung and Yüan Dynasties

(960 - 1350)

The transition from the Sung to Yüan dynasty can be
likened to a piece of music flowing from a humanistic world
to the beat of a militaristic empire. After Chao K'uang-yin
donned the dragon robes at Ch'en-ch'iao and became the
first emperor of the Sung dynasty (he is known to posterity
as T'ai-tsu), the chaos that had plagued China during the
Five Dynasties and Ten Kingdoms period following the
fall of the T'ang dynasty had come to an end. However,
it also opened a new era of conflict with the bordering
states of the Liao, Chin, and Western Hsia. Nevertheless,
the Sung dynasty continued to maintain and uphold the
essence of Chinese culture, bringing it to a golden age
as urban society and commercial activities flourished,
technological breakthroughs were made, and knowledge
spread rapidly through the land. Achievements in the
arts and crafts likewise reached new heights, and the
accomplishments of this dynasty became the model to
which later generations would aspire.

Elegance in Life

In the Sung dynasty, cultivated scholars and officials (known as the literati class) pursued a life of beauty just as refined as today's modern urbanites, if not more. The objects and materials used in their studios (such as paper, ink, brushes, and ink slabs), everyday implements (including utensils for the consumption of food, tea, and wine), and mirrors, pillows, and burners all reflected an emphasis on beauty and refinement sought among Sung upper classes. The arts of tasting tea, appreciating incense, arranging flowers, and hanging paintings for enjoyment had become a trend, filling the lives of literati with utmost beauty and elegance.

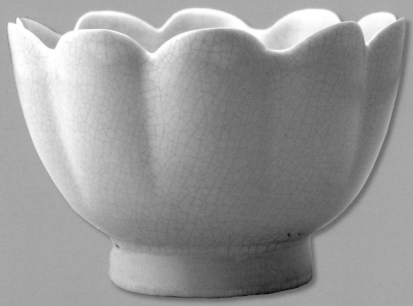

Warming bowl in the shape of a flower with light greenish-blue glaze, Porcelain, Ju ware, Northern Sung period

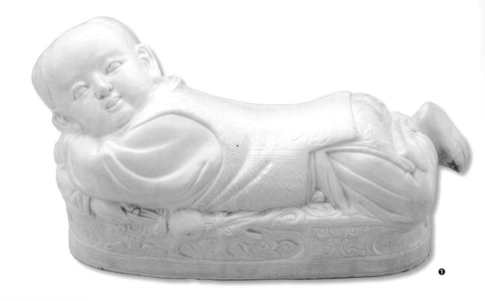

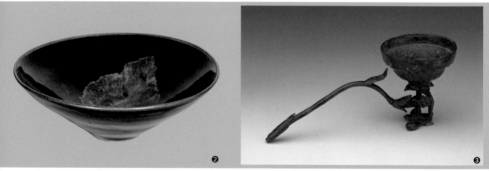

❶Pillow in the shape of a recumbent child with white glaze, Porcelain, Ting ware, Sung dynasty
Porcelain pillows in the shape of a child became widely popular in the Sung dynasty, due in part to the auspicious overtones of wishing for many children. This white porcelain pillow from the Ting kilns in Hopeh features fluid lines and a lively manner extremely pleasing to the eye.

❷Bowl with leaf pattern in black glazw, Porcelain, Chi-chou ware, Southern Sung period
The Sung witnessed the rise of the art and culture of tea, practitioners of which paid great attention to not only tea but also the implements used to make it. This tea bowl is decorated with a leaf pattern at the bottom highlighted against the dark glaze, creating a simple yet strikingly beautiful and natural touch.

❸Floral-shaped censer with handle, Bronze, Northern Sung period

Pursuing Revivalism

Hui-tsung, the ruler of the Northern Sung period, paid great attention to the establishment of new ceremonies and ritual objects based on systems used in antiquity, hoping to recreate the atmosphere of an idealized past. This also became part of a frenzy to collect and study ancient bronzes by scholars and members of the Sung court alike, a trend resulting in many imitations of ancient bronzes being made. In addition, it left behind several important catalogues, such as *Illustrated Research of Antiquities* and *Catalogue of [Hui-tsung's] Hsüan-ho Antiquities*, which became an important source of information in later archaistic pursuits.

Ting vessel with inscription of Cheng-ho period, Bronze, Northern Sung period
During the Cheng-ho reign of Emperor Hui-tsung, forms of bronze *ting* from the late Shang dynasty were imitated to create vessels that were given to high officials, who used them in sacrifices conducted in their family shrines.

The Beauty of Nature

One of the intellectual pursuits in the Sung dynasty derived inspiration from the myriad phenomena of nature, so various forms and features of the plant and animal world therefore came to be used to create many practical and aesthetically pleasing objects. This pursuit of beauty in nature is also found in the complementary qualities of perfection and naturalness found in Sung porcelains. For example, glaze is perfectly controlled to achieve a certain color, but it is allowed to drip in a natural way. Likewise, impurities in the glaze are tolerated for their irregular features when fired, and cracks in the glaze are appreciated for their natural beauty. These features all became objects of appreciation in many of the porcelains produced in this age.

Exchange with Foreign Cultures

The period of the Sung, Liao, Chin, and Yüan dynasties can be called one of the most important stages in the confluence of cultures in China. After the Khitan peoples of the north and the Jurchen of the northeast migrated into China proper, mutual exchange took place between their cultures and that of China, unfolding a new and extraordinary page in artistic interaction as well.

Bowl in black glaze with "hare's-fur" striations, Porcelain, Chien ware, Sung dynasty
"The light color of tea is suited to black cups" is an expression reflecting the aesthetics of dark-colored teacups prevalent in the Northern Sung period. The dark surface of this cup with its brownish striations has been compared to the color of a northern hare's fur and thus known as a "hare's-fur cup."

Crackled celadon stem bowl, Porcelain, Ko ware, Yüan dynasty

Pendant in the shape of a "fish-dragon", Jade, Liao dynasty
This "fish-dragon" form, with its dragon's head, fish body, and wings, originated with the Capricorn celestial form in Indian Buddhism. After being brought to China during the Sui and T'ang period, it became a popular motif on objects and pendants produced by peoples in the Liao and Chin dynasties.

The Sophistication and Spread of Porcelains

As kilns sprang up around China, the art of ceramics during the Sung and Yüan dynasties reveals a plethora of competing modes and manners. Dividing them on the basis of glaze color, the four major groups of white, celadon green, black, and mixed hues appear. With an ivory tinge to their glaze, Ting wares of Hopeh best represent white porcelains. The most fabulous celadons are represented by the uniquely warm and translucent yet meticulous blue-green glazes of Ju wares. There is also the light bluish glaze with ice-like crackle and dark rims of Kuan (or Official) wares. Lung-ch'üan wares, on the other hand, feature a translucent and stronger green glaze, Ko wares are covered with crackle, and Yao-chou wares have fluid yet strong, incised designs. The most renowned black wares are the ones from the Chien kilns in Fukien, while porcelains with mixed hues are perhaps best reflected by the colorful, dripping effects seen on Chün wares.

Narcissus basin with light greenish-blue glaze, Porcelain, Ju ware, Northern Sung
Ju ware, considered both now and in the past as the crowning achievement in Chinese ceramics, is epitomized by this perfect piece without the slightest crackle to its glaze.

Bowl with incised
three-fish decoration
in yellowish-green
glaze, Porcelain, Yao-
chou ware, Northern
Sung period

**Square ewer with appliqué mask and dragon-shaped handles in white glaze,
Porcelain, Ting ware, Northern Sung period**
Decorated with lotus blossom designs, two dragon-shaped handles and decorative
beast-head loops pasted in relief are done in imitation of ancient bronzes for an
elegant and classical quality.

**Vase with phoenix-shaped
handles in light greenish-blue
glaze, Porcelain, Lung-ch'üan
ware, Southern Sung period**
Except for the addition of the
decorative pair of phoenix handles,
the shape of this vessel follows that
from the Ju and Kuan kilns. The
upright yet elegant form, delicate
pastel color of the glaze, and purity
like that of jade make this an ideal
example of Lung-ch'üan ware.

Kuei **ritual vessel in light bluish-
green glaze, Porcelain, Kuan
ware, Southern Sung period**
The form of this celadon is similar to
that of a bronze *kuei* vessel from the
Western Chou dynasty. The inlay of
bronze along the rim and foot was
a popular Sung practice, and the
bluish-green celadon glaze is crackled
like ice and appears like an even slip
clinging to the form.

Planter with blue and violet glaze, Porcelain, Chün ware, Yüan dynasties
The rich colors and glossy surface of this piece stand out with hints of red and blue intermingling in the glaze with an irregular pattern. Known as "kiln change," this was a defining feature that later generations could not imitate.

The Early Ming Period (1350 - 1521)

Compared with the simple taste for the beauty of nature found in Sung dynasty arts and crafts, those of the Ming dynasty reveal a profusion of colors and forms for a completely different visual experience. Myriad forms of decoration were developed in workshops specially devoted to porcelains, lacquerware, and cloisonné enamelware at the Ming court between the reigns of the Hung-wu and Cheng-te Emperors. Official decorations and new glazes, combined with Cheng Ho's seven sailing missions through Southeast Asia and beyond, brought objects and ideas of China and the Middle East into much closer contact at this time–yielding a burst of mutual influence in the arts of the East and West for a great variety of forms and colors.

Underglaze Colors

Ching-te-chen kilns from the late Yüan dynasty and into the Hung-wu era of the early Ming began to develop the technique of underglaze colors. Either cobalt blue or copper red was used as a pigment under a transparent glaze to create a variety of patterns and designs in what became known as either underglaze blue ("blue and white") or underglaze red ("red and white"). The underglaze pigments on porcelains in this era tend to be thicker and feature iron dots for a deep, opulent effect.

After the Hung-wu era, underglaze blue porcelains gradually became the mainstream and reached a peak of production in the Yung-lo and Hsüan-te reigns. During this period, pigments for underglaze blue were imported from the Middle East. The higher iron content resulted in the formation of pure and colorful iron crystals. By the Ch'eng-hua and Hung-chih eras of the middle Ming dynasty, however, domestic cobalt from Lo-p'ing in Kiangsi was being used, giving the blue color grayish overtones for a lighter and more elegant atmosphere.

Bowl with underglaze copper red decoration of peony scrolls, Porcelain, Hung-wu reign, Ming dynasty
Underglaze red is achieved painting a design using a pigment with copper oxide as an ingredient, which is then covered with a transparent glaze and fired at high temperature. Large, thick forms for porcelains at this time are features following export wares produced previously in the Yüan dynasty.

Decoration featured not only landscape, figural, and bird-and-flower subjects, but also those related to Tibetan and Middle Eastern influences (in the form of Tibetan and Arabic script on the porcelains). Vessel shapes also included the "tankard," "flat *hu*," and "flower holder" done in imitation of silver and brass objects from areas to China's west. Such phenomena thus testify to the flourishing forms of exchange that took place between China and points west at this time.

Celestial global vase with underglaze blue decoration of dragon among lotus blossoms,
Porcelain, Yung-lo reign, Ming dynasty

The globular vase form with a round body is an innovation of the Yung-lo reign. The strong and sinuous dragon is seen here cavorting among a sea of winding lotus stems and blossoms that float and flicker across the surface of this vase to create a grand and majestic manner.

In addition to eye-catching underglaze
blue porcelains of the Hung-wu to
Cheng-te reigns, considerable progress
was also made at this time in other
glaze colors and overglaze techniques.
Examples adding to the fabulous array
of official Ming wares include "sweet
white" of the Yung-lo period and
"sacrificial red," "clear blue," "yellow
glaze," and green colors" of the Hsüan-
te era. Combinations of underglaze
blue and overglaze colors were also
gradually developed during the Ming
dynasty, such as *tou-ts'ai* ("competing
colors") of the Ch'eng-hua, *wu-ts'ai* ("five
colors") of the Chia-ching, and Wan-li
reigns, thus making the world of Ming
glaze colors even more vivacious.

❶Pair of saucepots in sacrificial red and cobalt blue
glaze with incised lotus petal, Porcelain, Hsüan-te
reign, Ming dynasty
The walls of the bodies here are decorated with four layers
of lotus petals in relief, making the vessels appear like lotuses
in bloom and giving them an innovative and refined touch.
❷Bowl with cobalt blue glaze decoration of white fish
and aquatic plants in a lotus pond, Porcelain, Hsüan-
te reign, Ming dynasty
❸Dish with overglaze decoration of fish and water
weeds in *wu-ts'ai* colors, Porcelain, Cheng-te reign,
Ming dynasty
❹Teacup with illustration of scholars outlined in
underglaze blue and filled in with *tou-ts'ai* colors,
Porcelain, Ch'eng-hua reign, Ming dynasty
This cup shows scenery that depicts literati enjoyments. The
underglaze cobalt-blue decoration and delineation in double
outlines was covered with transparent glaze and then red,
yellow, green, and ochre colors added to make the design
pure and eye-catching for a remarkably appealing work.

Stem bowl with underglaze blue decoration of waves, flying elephant and clouds, Porcelain, Hsüan-te reign, Ming dynasty

Official Vessel Types and Decoration

The private sector was strictly forbidden from copying or imitating the glaze colors, shapes, and decoration found on official Ming wares. The high-stemmed bowl, for example, was one of the common shapes among official Ming wares and such motifs as a flying beast with an elephant's head and a lion's body, the dragon, and sea beast also often adorn these porcelains.

Stem bowl with underglaze copper red decoration of three fruit, Porcelain, Hsüan-te reign, Ming dynasty

Covered jar with underglaze blue and overglaze in *tou-ts'ai* colors decoration of flying elephant above waves, Porcelain, C h'eng-hua reign, Ming dynasty

Carved red lacquer box with decoration of dragons and clouds, Hsüan-te reign, Ming dynasty

Carved Red Lacquer and Cloisonne Enamel

The Ming emperor Ch'eng-tsu, had the "Orchard Factory" official workshop established especially to produce the famous "picked red" carved lacquer that he admired. Layer upon layer of thin lacquer was added to gold, silver, tin, or wooden vessel forms to create a thickness suitable for carving. In the Ming dynasty, carving techniques matured as patterns were done with greater three-dimensional effect. In addition, the art form known as "cloisonné enamelware," which had originally come to China from the West via Eurasian channels opened previously during the Mongol Empire (and thus also called "Persian ware" or "foreign ware"), was being produced domestically by the early Ming.

Cloisonné enamel incense burner with decoration of lotus scrolls, Ming dynasty
The workshops at the Directorate of Imperial Accouterments in the Ming court were already able to produce filigree cloisonné enamelware, mostly in the form of patterns against a blue background. This being a flourishing period in its production, later generations would come to use the name "Ching-t'ai blue" to refer to this craft.

The Late Ming Period (1522 - 1644)

The foundations of the Ming rested on a tightknit centralized authority, but as the power of the dynasty weakened in later years, so did its authority. Nonetheless, handicrafts of the late Ming period rebounded rapidly in a decade of administrative reform by Chang Chü-cheng. At that time, various duties and labor requirements of artisans for the court could be paid off in cash, so the lack of skilled labor at official kilns naturally resulted in a decline in quality. Private kilns, on the other hand, witnessed rapid developments, working in tandem with the rise of industry and urban centers, which provided a source of professional labor and a market for their products. The various late Ming arts on display in this gallery represent the efforts and interaction of three factors at work in this era: the court, literati, and merchants.

The Rise of Colorful and Auspicious Patterns

With its colorfully glazed porcelains, lacquerware, and enamelware, arts and crafts of the Ming stand in strong contrast to the simple and archaic elegance of Sung dynasty taste. The effect all the more reveals the wealth and splendor of this age, especially the late Ming period, when porcelains with overglaze colors flourished. In this regard, *wu-ts'ai* (five-color) porcelains fired in the Chiaching and Wan-li reigns, for example, are unmatched in their splendor. Patterns and decorations on arts and crafts are even more abundant, symbolically auspicious objects and motifs associated with wealth, rank, and longevity being especially popular. Porcelains combining a profusion of colors with auspicious decoration show just how closely artistic tastes at this time reflected trends in life and the market.

Yellow-ground square basin with overglaze green decoration of phoenixes, Porcelain, Chia-ching reign, Ming dynasty

Gourd-shaped vase with underglaze blue decoration of cranes and deer, Porcelain, Chia-ching reign, Ming dynasty
The shape of a gourd is a metaphor for "fortune and rank" as well as "numerous descendants." Combined with the pine tree, crane, and symbol for the character "longevity," all of which represent long life, this object brims with auspicious overtones.

Garlic-shaped vase with decoration of dragon in *wu-ts'ai* colors, Porcelain, Wan-li reign, Ming dynasty

The top of this vase is like a bulbous head of garlic, and the thin neck is decorated with delicate motifs. The body is filled with a dragon among other motifs, painted in a straightforward yet free and lively manner, in marked contrast with previously neat and exacting styles.

Flowerpot in the shape of a sea-tortoise, Jade, Ming dynasty
Popular legend tells of "a carp jumping through Dragon Gate." Like an ordinary person who can become a lofty official, a lowly carp leaping through this pass becomes a great dragon. In fact, the head of the leaping carp here is shown sprouting horns as it transforms into a dragon, thus serving as a blessing for success.

Literati Archaic Trends

Archaic trends of literati emerged and came to dominate the art scene in the two to three centuries from the late Ming to the early Ch'ing dynasty. The scholarly pursuit of archaic elegance led to a strong desire for cultivation in connoisseurship. This trend also influenced the attitudes of many merchants and gentry who aspired to the same ideals, leading to widespread interest in antiquities. In response to this demand, a large quantity of replicas and imitations flooded the art market. As a result, one's collection (as well as its quantity and quality) became an indicator of taste and knowledge. Collectors also patronized artisans, contributing to a major rise in craftsmanship at this time.

Independent Craftsmen and Private Kilns

Commercial prosperity in late Ming society led to increasing numbers of craftsmen paying off obligatory service at official kilns to join the more lucrative private market. The quality of official wares naturally declined as the quantity of private wares quickly rose, the situation at private kilns in Ching-te-chen being the most obvious example. Artisans and literati also developed a fine level of cooperation at this time, the latter providing ideas as craftsmen used their refined techniques to produce exquisite objects. In fact, some outstanding artists gradually made a name for themselves via their distinctive works, thereby achieving considerable status in society. There was Lu Tzu-kang in jade carving circles and the great porcelain maker Chou Tan-ch'üan, whose works were highly prized by literati and collectors alike.

Yellow censer in the shape of a *ting*, mark of Chou Tan-ch'üan, Ming dynasty

Hu pot with dragons in white glaze, Porcelain, Te-hua ware, Ming dynasty
The Te-hua kilns, located in the province of Fukien, became renowned both domestically and abroad for the milky white porcelains they produced. This handled *hu*-pot is a typical Te-hua porcelain, featuring two sinuous dragons ingeniously worked into the design to form the spout and handle.

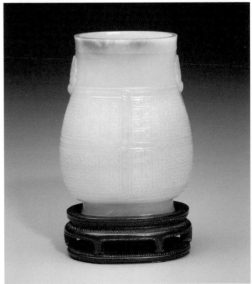

Jade water container with wooden base, mark of Li Wen-fu, Ming dynasty
The shape of this vessel follows that of the *hu* popular in the Warring States period, the body engraved with net-rope and hooked-cloud patterns.

The High Ch'ing Period (1662 - 1795)

The Ch'ing dynasty lasted for 268 years, but the period of 134 years spanning the reigns of the K'ang-hsi, Yung-cheng, and Ch'ien-lung Emperors is regarded as a time of particular prosperity in China. The fastidious attention paid by Manchu Ch'ing rulers to cultivating art and culture reveals their great vision. Starting from the K'ang-hsi reign, for example, the Ching-te-chen official kilns were re-established and palace workshops set up at the Yang-hsin Hall in the inner court. The Yung-cheng and Ch'ien-lung reigns continued the practice of having the court guide the production of crafts for imperial use, leading to great advances in traditional art forms. This was also a period when missionaries from Europe brought such innovative technological achievements as the latest in enamelware, chime clocks, and telescopes to the court. Trade items from Sinkiang in the far west, Tibet to the southwest, and Hindustan in northern India also had an enormous influence on the styles of objects produced at the Ch'ing court.

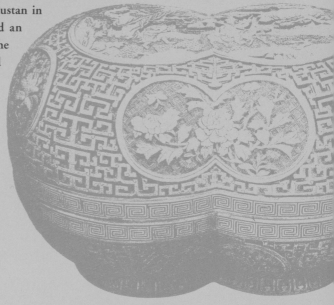

Manifestions of Boldness and Power

The official kilns at Ching-te-chen rose again in the K'ang-hsi era and starting from 1681 the court began sending officials there to oversee the production of porcelains. By the Yung-cheng and Ch'ien-lung era, standards for firing porcelains reached a peak, as unprecedented achievements were made in terms of the incredible glaze colors, richness of forms, and finesse of techniques. Imperial attention not only raised the level of porcelains, but also led to advances in techniques for carved red lacquerware and enamelware.

Vase with ruby red glaze, Porcelain, K'ang-hsi reign, Ch'ing dynasty
The moist and luscious ruby-red glaze here was achieved in imitation of Hsüan-te ware colors from the Ming dynasty.

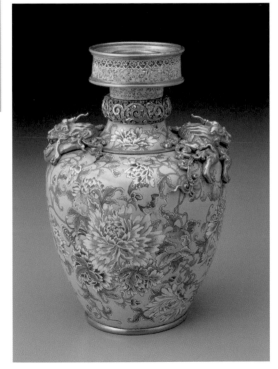

Metal vase with peony flowers and coiled dragons in painted enamels, Yung-cheng reign, Ch'ing dynasty
This domestically produced vase depicting a traditional Chinese design of peonies in painted enamels for a radiant display of colors. The sculptural gilt dragons on the shoulders also manifest the splendor of imperial grandeur at the Ch'ing court.

Exquisite Crafts of the Inner Court Workshops

The Palace Workshop in the Yang-hsin Hall at the Ch'ing court not only designed porcelains, it was also renowned for carvings in bamboo, wood, and ivory. As opposed to independent craftsmen of the late Ming period, most gifted craftsmen in this era were gathered either at court or in regional official workshops, these talents assembled to create works of unparalled technique and design for imperial use. For example, Ch'en Tsu-chang from Kwangtung was a master in ivory carving at the Palace Workshop during the Yung-cheng era, while Yang Wei-chan entered court service during the Ch'ien-lung reign and achieved such skill in wood carving as to receive praise from the emperor.

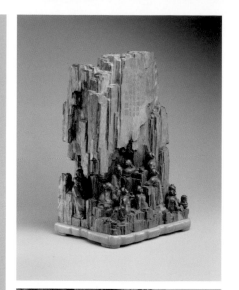

Aloeswood carving of the Nine Elders of Hsiang-shan, Yang Wei-chan, Ch'ing dynasty

Olive stone boat, Ch'en Tsu-chang, Ch'ing dynasty

Western Trends at the Court

From the late seventeenth and into the eighteenth century, Western missionaries wanted to bring Christianity to China, and respectfully submitting objects of tribute to the emperor in the Forbidden City was one of the best ways of doing so. Starting with the Italian missionary Matteo Ricci and the German missionary Johann Adam Schall von Bell in the Ming dynasty, such novel items as a chime clock were presented as tribute to the Wan-li Emperor. By the Ch'ing dynasty, the Belgian missionary Ferdinand Verbiest became an instructor for the K'ang-hsi Emperor and presided over the observatory at the Directorate of Astronomy. He also assisted in the *Complete Map of the Imperial Realm* marked in latitude and longitude. Western trends at the Ch'ing court came to have a strong impact on palace workshops, leading to artworks combining Eastern and Western styles.

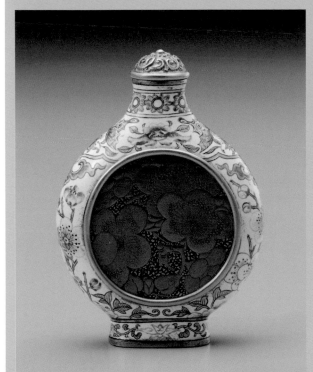

Portrait of the K'ang-hsi Emperor

Metal snuff bottle with decoration of plum-blossoms in painted enamels, K'ang-hsi reign, Ch'ing dynasty
The central panel of this snuff panel is decorated with plum blossoms rendered in gold lacquer, reflecting the Japanese *maki-e* decorative popular in Europe at the time. The combination with a traditional design of Chinese birds and flowers creates a new and interesting style.

Pair of gilt bronze pocket watches decorated with painted enamels, 18th century, European
The pocket watch, now considered a kind of antique, was one of the trendiest and most advanced objects in eighteenth-century China and popular among members of the Ch'ing imperial family and nobility.

Experiments, Revivals, and Innovations

In addition to their expertise in imitating antiques, master artisans of the High Ch'ing also created bold innovations. Through continuous experimentation, they were able to make forms completely different from those of the past. An example is the revolving vase produced at the official Ching-te-chen kilns in the eighteenth century. This ingenious design consists of a separate inner vase that can be revolved inside the outer form, creating a new way to appreciate porcelains. This innovation involves a complex structure with decoration designed accordingly and thus represents one of the high points in Ch'ing craftsmanship.

Vase with a rotating interior
and decoration of fish in cobalt
blue glaze, Porcelain, Ch'ien-lung
reign, Ch'ing dynasty
Special attention was placed in the
Ch'ien-lung reign on the production
of ingenious porcelain designs. This
revolving vase is actually composed of
two layers, one inside the other. The
outer wall consists of four openwork panels that
reveal patterns on the freely spinning inner
vase, which is decorated in famille rose with
aquatic plants, fallen leaves, and goldfish.
Spinning the neck of the vase makes the
goldfish on the inner vase appear to swim
among the plants, creating scenery that is
literally "moving."

The Late Ch'ing Period (1796 - 1911)

All eras of prosperity, no matter how good, must come to an end. For the Ch'ing dynasty, its power began to slip in the late eighteenth century. By the middle of the nineteenth century, corruption and intrigues in government combined with a failure to deal with encroaching Western powers resulted in both domestic upheaval and foreign conflict. The Ch'ing court faced unprecendented challenges and was forced to accept trends in modernization (but ultimately too little and too late). Taste in crafts of this period was no longer dictated by the court, but instead strongly represented public taste, thus reflecting the changes that were occurring at this time.

Splendor Bedazzling the Eye

The first impression people have of late Ch'ing art is splendor, in which sumptuous colors dazzle the eye to grab the attention of the viewer. This period also marked a grand synthesis of traditional decoration in handicrafts from the ages. The designs often appearing on works at this time include winding branches with leaves and blossoms, billowing clouds and rolling waves, and dragons in flight and phoenixes dancing about--all done in extraordinary detail. Perhaps the most famous official workshop was the "Ta-ya Studio," which is said to have produced works specifically for the imperial use of the Empress Dowager Tz'u-hsi. These objects are marked by a daring use of beautiful colors with designs comprised mainly of butterflies and birds and flowers against a backdrop of purple, blue, yellow, and green.

Box with overglaze flower and bird design on purple ground, *Ta-ya-chai* mark, Porcelain, Kuang-hsü reign, Ch'ing dynasty

Flaunting Techniques

As increasing numbers of official workshops closed down, many craftsmen turned to the private sector to make a living with their handiwork. They not only continued to pursue designs with great finesse, but also challenged themselves to develop ever more difficult techniques. The result is an astonishing variety of artworks. The collection of the National Palace Museum, for instance, includes an amazing set of concentric ivory openwork balls and an openwork handled ivory food carrier, both carved in incredible detail. Along with a small snuff bottle painted on the inside, these works demonstrate the painstaking effort of artisans in the late Ch'ing dynasty.

Four-tiered ivory box with openwork decoration, Ch'ing dynasty
The art of ivory carving flourished from the sixteenth to the eighteenth centuries, as large quantities of elephant ivory entered China at this time. This handled food container is composed of delicately carved panels of ivory depicting scenes of figures, animals, birds, vegetation, buildings, and boats, all done with such detail in openwork as to look like silk gauze. The handle is decorated with the Eight Immortals, adding an auspiciousness touch.

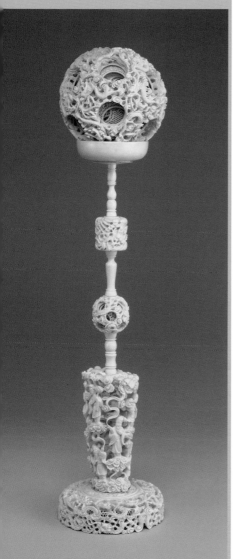

Glass snuff bottle with inner-painted traveling scene, painted by Chou Lo-yüan, Kuang-hsü reign, Ch'ing dynasty
A special, thin brush was used to reach inside the narrow mouth to paint the rustic scene shown on the inside of this glass snuff bottle, demonstrating that big things can come in small packages.

Set of concentric ivory balls with cloud-and-dragon design in openwork relief, Ch'ing dynasty
This set of ivory balls consists of at least 17 concentric layers, each of which moves freely and independently of the others. The carving of the design is also incredibly detailed, the level of precision demonstrated here amazing.

Auspicious motifs and designs have been appreciated in Chinese art since antiquity, and in the late Ch'ing it was no exception. Applications ranged widely, including everything from clothing to objects of daily life. Layer upon layer of complex patterns dealing with auspicious subject matter not only give works a sumptuousness but also function as a blessing for good luck.

Dish with dragon and phoenix design on green ground, Porcelain, Ching-te-chen ware, Chia-ch'ing reign, Ch'ing dynasty

Vase with decoration of a hundred butterflies painted in overglaze enamels, Porcelain, Ching-te-chen ware, Kuang-hsü reign, Ch'ing dynasty
Butterflies, symbols of prosperity and longevity, appear in every color and form as they fill the surface of this vase for an imperially magnificent effect.

The Art of Calligraphy and Painting

Calligraphy and painting reflect two facets of the traditional world of fine arts in Chinese culture, since both involve use of the same tool–the brush. Calligraphic lines and dots also make up one of the fundamental features of painting, hence the ancient saying that "painting and calligraphy spring from the same well." This therefore emphasizes the exceptionally close relationship between calligraphy and painting in Chinese culture.

The works of calligraphy and painting in the National Palace Museum derive for the most part from the collections of the Sung, Yüan, Ming and Ch'ing courts, including many classic works by ancient masters throughout the ages. Works of calligraphy and painting, due to their fragile nature, cannot be displayed for extended periods of time and thus must be rotated every three months or so, presented in permanent and special exhibitions from the collection. Both preserving and displaying these masterpieces of the brush from Chinese history allow them to be shared and appreciated by people now and in the future.

Late Greenery of Autumn Mountains (detail), Kuan T'ung, Five Dynasties period

Calligraphy

Calligraphy, the art of writing, has a long history in China that can be traced as far back as the oracle bone and bronze scripts of the Shang and Chou dynasties. These forms gradually developed into types known as large and small seal scripts as well as clerical script. Cursive, regular, and running scripts emerged by the Eastern Han dynasty and Wei and Chin period. Writing is not only a tool to record events and transmit ideas, but the aesthetic rendering and spacing of characters has also long been admired as one of the hallmarks of Chinese culture.

Elegance of the Wei and Chin

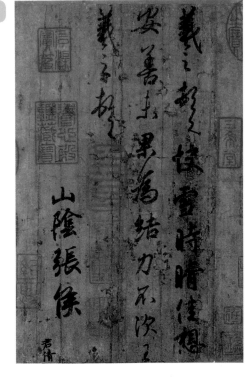

The period after the Han dynasty and before the Sui dynasty is one of the greatest in terms of changes that took place among script forms in Chinese calligraphy. Nobility and gentry of the Eastern Chin, for example, advocated the elegant pursuits of life and paid special attention to refinement in calligraphy. The running and cursive scripts of the great calligrapher Wang Hsi-chih reached a level of perfection to which later calligraphers aspired, for which Wang became known as the "Sage of Calligraphy."

Clearing after Snow, Wang Hsi-chih, Chin Dynasty
This piece of calligraphy was originally a letter that Wang Hsi-chih had written to a friend. The archaic simplicity of the brushwork reveals a naturally reserved yet effortlessly fluid harmony.

Methods of the T'ang

The calligraphic mainstream in the early T'ang dynasty was regular script, in which attention was placed on stroke methods and formal structure. By the High T'ang period, cursive script also came to dominate calligraphic circles, reflecting a spirit of freedom and romanticism pursued in upper-class society of the time and perhaps best represented by the expressive brushwork of Sun Kuo-t'ing. By the mid-T'ang period, cursive script developed even further into so-called "wild cursive," its most famous practitioners being Huai-su and Chang Hsü. Meanwhile, Yen Chen-ch'ing and Liu Kung-ch'üan set foundations for the norms and models of regular script. Thus, by this time, the features of the various script types in Chinese calligraphy had already been well-established.

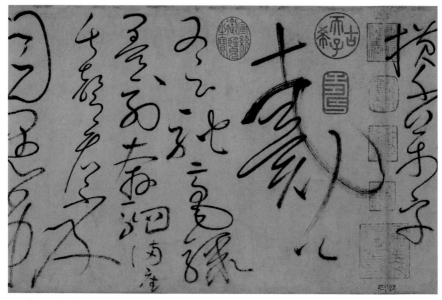

Autobiography (detail), Huai-su, T'ang dynasty
Free and easy by nature, Huai-su would often do a piece of calligraphy in a drunken state, bringing the wildness of cursive script to its limit of legibility.

Personalities of the Sung

Sung dynasty calligraphy focused on personal feelings, the pursuit of ideas, and expressions beyond the ordinary. Running script, best suited for the breadth of emotions, flourished the most among literati at this time. Ts'ai Hsiang, Su Shih, Huang T'ing-chien, and Mi Fu, known as the "Four Masters of the Northern Sung," each had their distinctive form of expression, making them some of the most representative figures in Sung dynasty calligraphy.

Sung dynasty emperors also showed a keen appreciation for calligraphy. Emperor Hui-tsung, in particular, developed a new form known as "slender gold script," noted for its unique forcefulness and elegance.

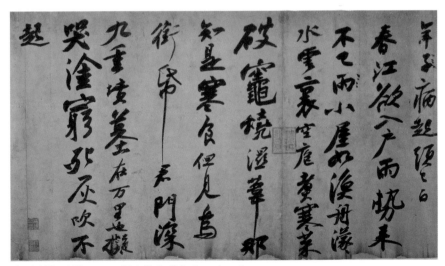

The Cold Food Observance (detail), Su Shih, Sung dynasty
Su Shih did this work after having been banished by the court to Huang-chou (modern Huang-kang, Hupeh). A work written during a low in his life, the characters rise and fall with his emotions as forms fluctuate in response. The combined beauty of poetry and calligraphy has made this a premier example among Su Shih's surviving works.

On Szechwan Silk (detail), Mi Fu, Sung dynasty
Special Szechwan silk, noted for its exceptional purity and fine weave, was treasured for painting and calligraphy. Mi Fu did this work at the age of 37, in the prime of his life. With exceptionally fluid and free brushwork, Mi Fu's force reveals considerable variety where the tip of the brush is exposed, creating a sparkling effect as it was flicked across the silk.

Revivalism of the Yüan

With the strong advocacy of the great artist Chao Meng-fu, Yüan dynasty calligraphy turned against the expressive ideas of Sung calligraphers towards greater reverence for the ancient methods of the Chin and T'ang. In this trend of revivalism, the main developments took place in running and cursive scripts.

Chao Meng-fu's calligraphy is known for its exceptional elegance and beauty, his regular script comparable to that of the T'ang masters Yen Chen-ch'ing, Liu Kung-ch'üan, and Ou-yang Hsün—so much that the four are often called the "Four Masters of Regular Script." As a result, Chao Meng-fu had a great influence on calligraphers of the Yüan and early Ming dynasty.

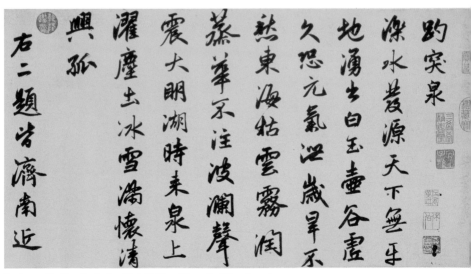

Poetry on the Pao-t'u Spring (detail), Chao Meng-fu, Yüan dynasty

Modelbooks and Steles of the Ming and Ch'ing

In the middle Ming dynasty, such Soochow literati as Chu Yün-ming and Wen Cheng-ming not only pursued styles of the Chin and T'ang dynasties, they also emphasized personal forms of expression. The great late-Ming connoisseur and painter-calligrapher Tung Ch'i-ch'ang also had an enormous impact on theoretical and calligraphic developments of the late Ming and early Ch'ing.

Ch'ing dynasty calligraphy can generally be divided between adherents of the Modelbook School and those of the Stele School. Such Modelbook School calligraphers as Liu Yung followed the tradition of Sung, Yüan, and Ming dynasty modelbooks. Followers of the Stele School, on the other hand, were quite interested in inscriptions found on ancient and unearthed bronze vessels and stone steles. These calligraphers derived inspiration from the simple yet majestic forms of seal and clerical scripts on bronzes and steles, and this innovative trend eventually came to the forefront.

Seven-character Regulated Verse (detail), Chu Yün-ming, Ming dynasty

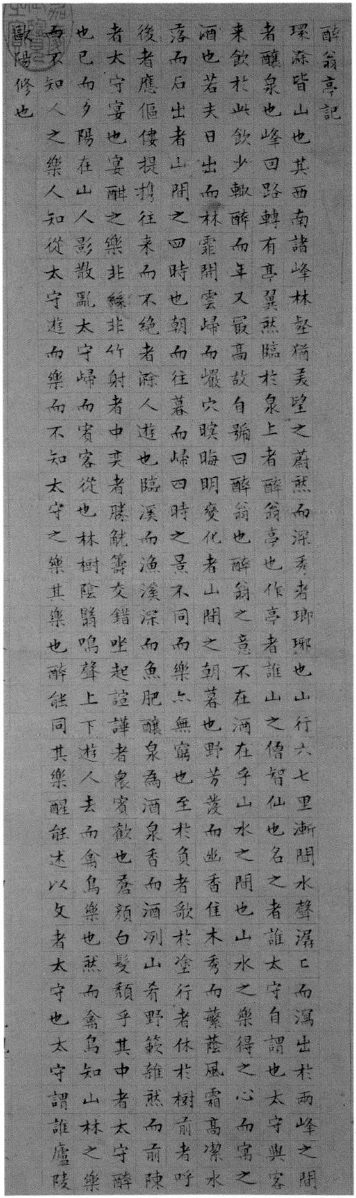

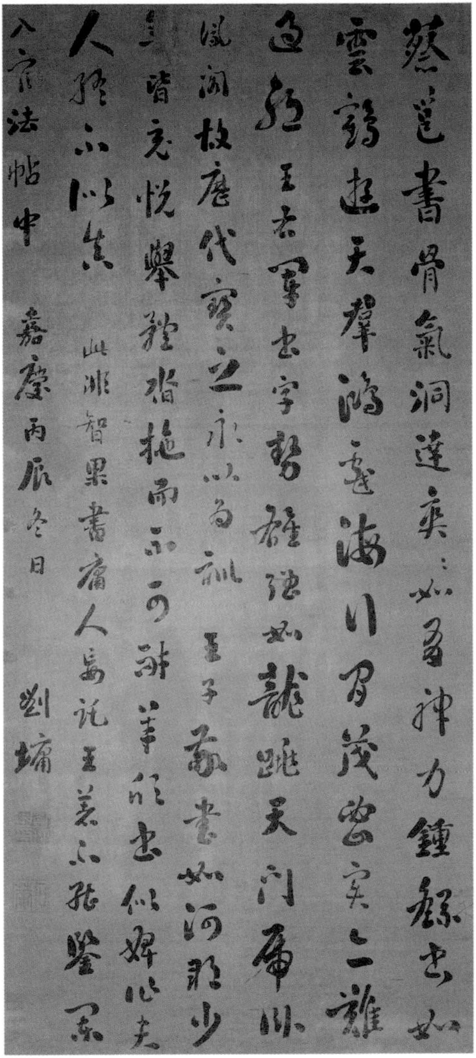

慈旨書骨氣洞達，爽爽如有神力。鍾繇書如雲鵠遊天，群鴻戲海，行間茂密，實亦難過於王右軍。書字勢雄強，如龍跳天門，虎臥鳳闕，故歷代寶之，永以為訓。王子敬書如河……美皆亢悅，舉體遒健，挺拔而不可……筆力……少夫人研不似真。

山濤智果書備人品記王……八分法帖中

嘉慶丙辰冬日

劉墉

Copy from the Ch'un-hua Modelbooks, Liu Yung, Ch'ing dynasty

醉翁亭記

環滁皆山也。其西南諸峰，林壑尤美，望之蔚然而深秀者，琅琊也。山行六七里，漸聞水聲潺潺而瀉出於兩峰之間者，釀泉也。峰回路轉，有亭翼然臨於泉上者，醉翁亭也。作亭者誰？山之僧智仙也。名之者誰？太守自謂也。太守與客來飲於此，飲少輒醉，而年又最高，故自號曰醉翁也。醉翁之意不在酒，在乎山水之間也。山水之樂，得之心而寓之酒也。

若夫日出而林霏開，雲歸而巖穴暝，晦明變化者，山間之朝暮也。野芳發而幽香，佳木秀而繁陰，風霜高潔，水落而石出者，山間之四時也。朝而往，暮而歸，四時之景不同，而樂亦無窮也。

至於負者歌於塗，行者休於樹，前者呼，後者應，傴僂提攜，往來而不絕者，滁人遊也。臨溪而漁，溪深而魚肥，釀泉為酒，泉香而酒洌，山肴野蔌，雜然而前陳者，太守宴也。宴酣之樂，非絲非竹，射者中，弈者勝，觥籌交錯，起坐而喧嘩者，眾賓歡也。蒼顏白髮，頹然乎其中者，太守醉也。

已而夕陽在山，人影散亂，太守歸而賓客從也。樹林陰翳，鳴聲上下，遊人去而禽鳥樂也。然而禽鳥知山林之樂，而不知人之樂；人知從太守遊而樂，而不知太守之樂其樂也。醉能同其樂，醒能述以文者，太守也。太守謂誰？廬陵歐陽修也。

Record of the Pavilion of the Old Drunk, Wen Cheng-ming, Ming dynasty

Painting

The major subjects in Chinese painting are landscapes, birds-and-flowers, and figures. Influenced by traditional philosophy, artists not only were stimulated to pursue outer appearances, but also to lay stress on the inner nature and harmony of things. The two mutual concerns of "spirit harmony creating life" (the inner world) and "the structural methods of brushwork" (the outer world) became important critical norms in Chinese art. Literati painters, in fact, even came to link the ephemeral, personal world of the artist with the objects rendered, forming a counterbalance to the other great tradition in Chinese art history—tastes in professional painting led by the court.

The T'ang Dynasty

The open, lyrical side to T'ang society led to a flourishing era marked by various forms of cultural exchange and fusion. This was a time when figural subjects dominated painting, including many renderings of ladies and their activities. The figure painter Wu Tao-tzu of Buddhist and Taoist subjects during this period was also revered as the "Sage of Painting." As for landscapes, both monochrome ink renditions and the resplendent colors of the "blue-and-green landscape" and "gold-and-green landscape" traditions co-existed.

A Palace Concert, anonymous, T'ang dynasty
Depicted here is a group of palace ladies enjoying music in a work featuring beautiful colors and delicate brush tones.

The Five Dynasties Period

Despite the chaos of the Five Dynasties period, this was also a time of great advances in the arts. The Southern T'ang and Western Shu emerged as cultural centers, and the painting academy established at the Southern T'ang court became the forerunner of the academy system later under the Sung dynasty.

Bird-and-flower painter was mainly divided into two schools—the more refined and opulent, fine-line manner of Huang Ch'üan featuring outlines filled with colors, in contrast to the more rustic and untrammeled style of Hsü Hsi with monochrome ink and light color washes. Both developments would have a significant influence on later bird-and-flower painting.

In landscape painting, Ching Hao and Kuan T'ung in the north emphasized the structure and texture of mountain forms, while Tung Yüan and Chü-jan represented the southern landscape style with its focus on rendering the atmosphere of misty and water-filled Kiangnan.

Layers of Crags and Clusters of Trees, Chü-jan, Five Dynasties period

The Sung Dynasty

By the Sung dynasty, landscapes finally emerged as the dominant subject in Chinese painting. Such Northern Sung artists as Li Ch'eng, Fan K'uan, and Kuo Hsi as well as the Southern Sung artists Li T'ang, Liu Sung-nien, Ma Yüan, and Hsia Kuei represented the general trend from large, full-scale monumental representations of mountains to more intimate and edited worlds focusing on the lyrical balance of solid (landscape) and void (water and sky). The sense of space created by Sung dynasty landscape painters came to reflect the idealized natural world in the minds of people at the time.

The painting academy established at the Sung dynasty court specialized in the cultivation and training of professional artists, becoming the center of creativity for painting in the nation. This was especially so under the meticulous attention of Emperor Hui-tsung, a painter and calligrapher himself, leading to rapid developments in all subject matter. In particular, the contemplative nature of bird-and-flower painting reached a pinnacle of achievement at this time.

The great Sung poet Su Shih, along with such literati as Wen T'ung and Mi Fu, developed such themes related to the scholar as withered trees, bamboo, and stones as well as plum blossoms and orchids. These figures thus eventually became regarded as pioneers in the important tradition of literati painting in China.

Travelers Among Mountains and Streams, Fan K'uan, Sung dynasty

Bamboo in Monochrome Ink, Wen T'ung, Sung dynasty

Immortal in Splashed Ink, Liang K'ai, Sung dynasty

The Yüan Dynasty

China in the Yüan dynasty was ruled by the Mongols as part of their vast empire. With lowered social status and restrictions on the pursuing an official career for many ethnic Chinese, Yüan literati often chose to live in reclusion instead, expressing their feelings and ideas through poetry, calligraphy, and painting. In the latter, this led to descriptions of solitude and distance with a more personal manner, creating untrammeled landscape styles of purity and reclusion.

❶

❷

The Ming Dynasty

Academic painting at the court in the early Ming dynasty mainly followed the tradition of the Southern Sung painting academy. Later the "Che School," represented by painters from the Chekiang and Fukien region, rose to prominence in the art scene with its forceful and sometimes wild brushwork. Afterwards, such "Wu School" painters as Shen Chou and Wen Cheng-ming from the Kiangsu area pursued the styles of the Four Yüan Masters.

By the late Ming dynasty, Tung Ch'i-ch'ang had become the leader of literati painting circles, achieving a grand synthesis in both the theory and practice of painting. Bird-and-flower painting of this period developed mostly along the lines of the splashed-ink sketching-ideas painting style, represented by such artists as Hsü Wei and Ch'en Ch'un.

The Ch'ing Dynasty

❶Kublai Khan Hunting (detail), Liu Kuan-tao, Yüan dynasty

❷Dwelling in the Fu-ch'un Mountains (detail), Huang Kung-wang, Yüan dynasty This detail from a long handscroll depicts scenery along the shores of the Fu-yang River. The rhythmic brushwork produces many variations as river and mountains are pulled up close at times, and at others seen from a distance, leading to a wide array of spatial contexts. An important representative of Yüan literati landscape painting, Huang Kung-wang, along with Wu Chen, Ni Tsan, and Wang Meng, became known as one of the Four Yüan Masters.

The tradition of landscape painting in the early Ch'ing dynasty followed the stylistic precedent established by Tung Ch'i-ch'ang in the late Ming. Several of the representative painters of this "Orthodox School" went by the surname Wang and thus known as the "Four Wangs" (Wang Shih-min, Wang Chien, Wang Hui, and Wang Yüan-ch'i). This was also a period of painters "left over" from the Ming dynasty who either became Buddhists or led a more reclusive life--they were known as the "Four Monks" (Pa-ta shan-jen, Shih-t'ao, Shih-hsi, and Chien-chiang). In addition, Kung Hsien of the "Eight Masters of Nanking" appeared at this time.

The greatest innovations in the middle Ch'ing dynasty took place in the works of the so-called "Eight Eccentrics of Yangchow." The rise of regional developments marked late Ch'ing painting, including the Shanghai School and Lingnan School. Artists not only sought a foundation in literati painting, but also pursued the ideals of the Four Perfections of poetry, calligraphy, painting, and seal carving. The fusion of literary elegance and down-to-earth tastes paved the way for new realms of traditional Chinese painting in modern times.

Lofty Mount Lu, Shen Chou, Ming dynasty

Shady Trees in a Summer Landscape,
Tung Ch'i-ch'ang, Ming dynasty

Peonies (detail), Yün Shou-p'ing, Ch'ing dynasty

A Hundred Steeds (detail), Lang Shih-ning (Giuseppe Castiglione), Ch'ing dynasty

Shedding Light on History

Highlights of Ch'ing Historical Documents

Gems in the Rare Books Collection

Religious Sculpture

Arts from the Ch'ing Imperial Collection

Splendors of Ch'ing Furniture

Highlights of Ch'ing Historical Documents

The collection of the National Palace Museum includes more than 400,000 Ch'ing dynasty documents and archives. These offer important first-hand glimpses into the consolidation and glorious rule of the High Ch'ing, the struggles for power and conflicts that later marred the political scene, and finally the decline that culminated in the end of the imperial system in China. The exhibitions here are divided into four parts: "Imperial Mandates: Proclamations of the Emperor," "Official Books and Annals," "Memorials, Record Copies, and Archive Volumes," and "Documents on Taiwan Aborigines." These fragile objects made mostly of paper are rotated every three months to preserve them for posterity.

Imperial Mandates: Proclamations of the Emperor

Edicts generally known as "imperial mandates" come in many different forms. They often begin with the phrase, "The Emperor, who governs with the Mandate of Heaven, declares that..." and end as "Proclaimed to all under the Heavens, let it be known." The specific contents in between would be written in both Manchu and Chinese. "Imperial patents of nobility" were presented to meritorious officials and often done in handscroll format, leaving enough space at the end for descendants who inherited the title to have their names written. *Piao* and *ch'ien*, edicts, and credentials were issued as part of relations with countries of lower standing and with Western powers. These documents are thus vital primary sources of information for understanding international relations at the Ch'ing court.

Proclamation of the personal rule of the T'ung-chih Emperor, February 23, 1873
Since the T'ung-chih Emperor assumed the throne at the tender age of five, the Empress Dowager Tz'u-hsi administered the affairs of state from behind the scenes and thereby came to hold great power. This proclamation of 1873 was intended to inform everybody that the emperor was personally assuming power. However, he could not shake the image of a puppet emperor and died the following year of illness, his rule lasting for less than two years.

Official Books and Annals

The Ch'ing court paid special attention to the compilation of official history, which is why it left behind a large number of documentary and historical books. These even include materials before the Manchu conquered China (represented by the "Archives in Old Manchu") as well as such compilations as "Archives of the Diary Keeper," "Veritable Records of the Emperors," and "Biographies."

Memorials, Record Copies, and Archive Volumes

Memorials were documents intended as a means of communication between the emperor and high officials. After the emperor personally read a memorial sent from an official, he would use red ink to write his response in what was known as a "vermilion rescript." In addition to the originals themselves, the secretarial institution of the Ch'ing court, known as the "Council of State," kept copies of all such vermilion rescripted memorials, called "record copies." The archives assembled and organized by the Council of State into transcribed volumes form a rich source of history known as "archived volumes."

Court Diary Volumes, 1807
The National Palace Museum collection includes archives of the emperor's diary keeper from 1672 up to the end of the dynasty in 1911. The contents record every detail of the emperor's daily life, ranging from everything done at work and rest (including what he ate and drank) to his meetings with officials and management of court and country.

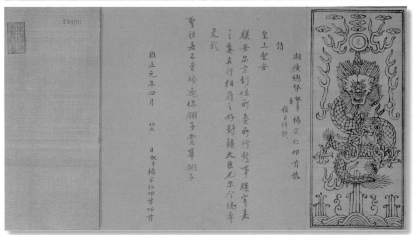

Memorial wishing the emperor well from the Governor-general of Hu-Kwang, Yang Tsung-jen

Documents on Taiwan Aborigines

Documents and archives from the Ch'ing court now in the National Palace Museum include much information on Taiwan, such as maps of Taiwan, images of aborigines, and memorials written by the Governor of Taiwan and the Governor-general of Fukien-Chekiang. These offer a better understanding of Taiwan geographically as well as the features and customs of its inhabitants at the time.

Illustrated Official Tribute to the Imperial Ch'ing, written on imperial commission by Fu Heng, et al., Ch'ien-lung reign

Gems in the Rare Books Collection

The National Palace Museum holds roughly 200,000 volumes of antique books. In addition to coming from the collection of the former Ch'ing court, other sources include a significant set of Chinese books purchased in Japan by Yang Shou-ching at the end of the Ch'ing dynasty as well as various donations, comprising many rare copies. All of these, in fact, are important for learning more about the history of book production in China. The exhibitions on rare books are divided into two categories, "Understanding Rare Books" and "Appreciating Rare Books," not only in the hope that visitors can study these texts but also discover their inherent beauty.

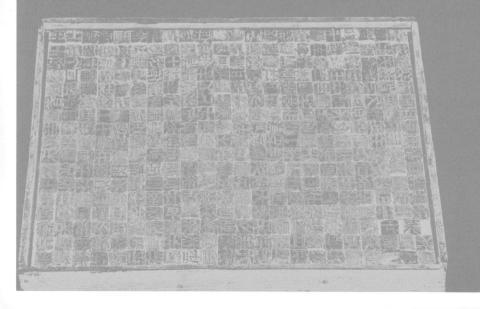

Understanding Rare Books

When mentioning books, the first thing that comes to mind is the development of printing. The technique of carving blocks of wood to create characters for printing emerged in the T'ang dynasty, with advances made in the Sung. In the Northern Sung, Pi Sheng invented movable print in clay, and the production of books became even more convenient. However, the main form of printed books in China remained woodblock carving, with the addition of color print techniques later on. The publishing industry flourished in the Sung dynasty, as the government, private individuals, and bookshops all printed books. In the Ming and Ch'ing dynasties, the government with its vast resources focused even more energy on editing books. The efforts of such official institutions for publishing as the Directorate of Ceremonial in the Ming dynasty and the Wu-ying Palace printing office in the Ch'ing dynasty became a model for private industry.

There was also the question of how to categorize all these books, a field of learning all by itself. The famous "Complete Library of the Four Treasuries" used the categories of the Classics, history, philosophy, and collectanea, which became the representative method of classifying books in traditional China.

Imperially Endorsed Complete Library of the Four Treasuries, Wen-yüan Pavilion edition, Ch'ien-lung reign, Ch'ing dynasty

Illustrated Edition of the Book of Odes, Handwritten by Emperor Ch'ien-lung, Ch'ing dynasty

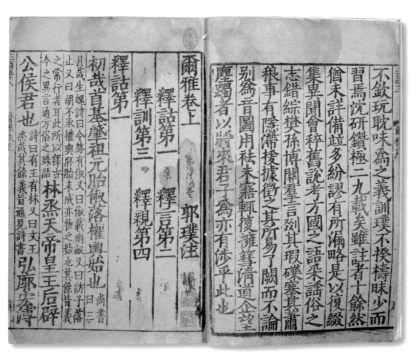

Erh-ya, annotated by Kuo P'u (Chin dynasty), Directorate of Education edition, Southern Sung period

Appreciating Rare Books

The appreciation of Chinese rare books can take the form of print type, binding, or illustrations. After woodblock carving emerged, many printers emulated the styles of famous calligraphers. These became known, for example, as the Yen Style (after Yen Chen-ch'ing), Liu Style (after Liu Kung-ch'üan), and Chao Style (after Chao Meng-fu). By the Ming dynasty, a special type of print known as "Sung print type" evolved, featuring elongated characters that made them easier to carve and thus widely used. The binding of ancient books went from bound bamboo slats and silk cloth to the use of paper, either as scrolls, or in accordion mounting, or finally in the more universal format known as stitched binding. Accommodating different materials, binding methods made it easier for readers as greater attention was also placed on the cover and packaging for aesthetic reasons. The addition of illustrations likewise spurred greater interest in books. Pictures in print originally emerged mainly to illustrate Buddhist scriptures, but later texts and historical stories, novels, and dramas were illustrated not only to inform but also as a means to appeal to readers.

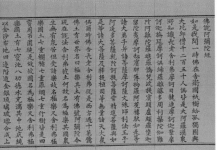

The Amitabha Sutra, translated by Kumarajiva, Ch'in dynasty (Yao)

漢史紀宣帝時詔諸儒講五經同異蕭望
之等評奏其議上親稱制臨決焉乃立梁
邱易大小夏侯尚書穀梁春秋博士
解易西漢史上記宣帝好文見五經所
言都是修身治天下的大道理自經秦
人燒燬一番到今表章之後雖已漸次
尋出但諸儒傳授互有異同不得歸一定
而諸家傳註亦且各以為是無一定
之說因此詔諸臣講究五經同異如
經文有不同的便要見某人說誰是真傳誰說
錯誤傳註有不同的便與經旨相悖又
與經旨相合某人說的每講究而裁決其是誰
命蕭望之等評論他每講究而裁決其
非奏聞於上上親制臨視而裁決其
可否這五經中定以先儒梁邱賀傳授
的易經夏侯勝夏侯建傳授的尚書穀
梁的易經立博士之官著他教習弟子以廣
經各立博士之官蓋先已有定論故不
其傳其詩禮二經蓋先已有定論故不
述也自宣帝以來五經如日中天傳之
萬世為治天下者之準則其功亦大矣

Illustrated Lessons from Imperial History, Illustrated Lessons from Imperial History, edited by Chang Chü-cheng (Ming dynasty); illustrated by Shen Chen-lin, handwritten by P'an Tsu-yin and others (Ch'ing dynasty), red-line Imperial Household edition, Ch'ing dynasty

To instruct the young emperor Shen-tsung, a Ming dynasty court official compiled a collection of stories about emperors from Chinese history, dating back to the legendary Emperors Yao and Shun. Each of these stories, 117 in all, included a finely rendered illustration intended to capture the young ruler's fancy as he learned about the contents. The version now in the National Palace Museum is a handwritten edition with color paintings produced at the Ch'ing inner court, including now only 56 of the stories.

Religious Sculpture

Buddhism emerged in India in the fifth century BCE and gradually spread across Asia, encompassing many areas to become a cross-cultural religious phenomenon. In China, Buddhism merged with native thought and beliefs to form a religion different from that originally appearing in India. As for Buddhist art, a variety of different styles also resulted. The golden quality of gilt bronze sculptures, for example, became an important medium for the spread of Buddhism, both propagating religious content and also valued for aesthetic reasons in its own right.

Tibetan Buddhist Art

Buddhism made its way from India into Tibet starting around the seventh century CE, gradually merging with native culture to become the unique regional form known as "Tibetan Buddhism." Artistic styles with strong influences from Kashmir, eastern India, Nepal, and Tunhuang led to the formation of Tibetan modes of expression that made their way into China and merged with Chinese manners, especially after the fifteenth century. Generally speaking, Tibetan Buddhist sculpture reached a peak during the fourteenth to eighteenth centuries. Compared to solemn Buddha figures frequently appearing in Chinese renderings, Tibetan images sometimes stand out for their fierce appearance or coupled male and female figures.

The Northern Dynasties to Sui and T'ang

Buddhism spread rapidly in China from the late third to late sixth century CE. With imperial sponsorship, a great number of Buddhist scriptures were translated, gilt bronze sculptures cast, and caves with images created, bringing Buddhist art to an unprecedented level in China. Generally speaking, Buddhist sculptures of the Northern Wei feature a more simple and awkward style that still is imposing nonetheless, while the manner of the Southern Dynasties tends to be more elegant and refined.

Mahakala, Gilt bronze, 15th c.
Gonpo, known as Mahakala in Sanskrit, originally was an incarnation of the Hindu deity Shiva, but later became one of the eight great protectors of Tibetan Buddhism. Since traveling merchants often placed an image of Gonpo in their tents, this figure became known as the "Tent-protecting Spirit."

Contact with India rose dramatically by the Sui and especially in the T'ang period. After a period of adaptation and fusion, Indian Buddhism had become thoroughly sinicized, inaugurating a golden era of "Chinese Buddhism" that also witnessed spread into Japan and Korea. The subject matter of Buddhist art in this period also was enriched enormously, as the forms of Buddhist figures became more voluptuous and bold.

Shakyamuni Buddha, Northern Wei dynasty
The solemn appearance of this Buddha is complemented by a flaming, finely rendered body halo. The front is composed of flames and seven buddhas, while the back is divided into three levels, depicting scenes from Buddhist scriptures. Despite the small size, it nonetheless reflects the serenity and nobility of this figure.

The Sung to Ch'ing Dynasties

After the Five Dynasties period, Buddhism increasingly became a part of peoples' lives. And with the development and spread of printing techniques in the Sung dynasty, Buddhist scriptures became widespread among the populace. Buddhist sculptures made at this time are mostly fine and beautifully elegant. By the Ming and Ch'ing dynasties, Buddhism's presence in Chinese society stabilized and was marked by fewer innovations. Buddhist sculptures from this era are often beautifully and meticulously rendered, focusing on decoration with a greater emphasis on popular culture.

Avalokiteshvara Bodhisattva holding a child, Gilt bronze, Ming dynasty
In response to popular beliefs, many types of Kuan-yin images appeared during the Ming dynasty. These include Kuan-yin holding a child, which became an iconic figure for those wishing to have children.

Avalokiteshvara Bodhisattva, Gilt bronze, Sung dynasty

Arts from the Ch'ing Imperial Collection

The vast majority of objects in the National Palace Museum come from the collections of the Ch'ing dynasty court. This exhibition hopes to reveal the quality of the former Ch'ing collections, with the design of the display contents intended to reflect both image and substance. The image portion involves the display of a curio box, which symbolizes the depth and breadth of Ch'ing collecting in miniature form while also reflecting a rich cultural heritage and a mode of life and appreciation. The substance portion includes a wide array of display items that allow viewers to understand the great tradition and importance of collecting objects in the Chinese system of values. The exhibit also deals with the various sources of the Ch'ing court collection, its means of organizing and managing the objects, and the new significance it gave to the pieces in its possession. There is also an analysis from the perspective of imperial taste in objects and its influences. Through these four subcategories audiences will hopefully be able to understand the significance of these once private imperial artworks, the beauty of which can now be shared by people all over the world.

Passion for Collecting, Space for Amusement

The exteriors of curio boxes are often beautifully decorated and their contents equally amazing. Masterpieces of design and skill, they come in a variety of forms that have been called "toy chests of the emperor."

天球合璧
上層
端研
御臨王帖冊
唐岱秋山邨屋軸

Curio box with filled-in gold and lacquered dragon-and phoenix décor (containing 44 curios), Ch'ien-lung reign, Ch'ing dynasty
Curio boxes were often named by the emperor himself; this one, for example, was called "Celestial Sphere for a Perfect Match." The box includes a list of the various curios inside and is divided according by level, providing for a clear account.

The Origins of the Collection Objects

Objects in the Ch'ing court collections come from many sources. They include both works inherited from previous imperial courts and a large number of objects produced by the court workshops or presented as tribute by officials. There are gifts from foreign lands that not only add an exotic touch to the collection, but are also often related to important political events that make them historically important as well.

"Myriad Cycles" sandalwood curio box (with jade carvings of the twelve zodiac animals, jade case, and Yung Yen's album of calligraphy, Ch'ien-lung reign, Ch'ing dynasty
This box of jades was presented as tribute by Ch'üan Te, the Soochow Superintendent of Imperial Silk Manufacturing. Although not a very lofty position, it did command considerable resources, and many of the objects presented by officials in this position to the court were precious.

The Preservation and Collection of Artifacts

The court in the High Ch'ing period paid great attention to the collection of objects in its care. It employed a clear system of management, individualized methods of packaging, clever means of restoration to give objects new life, and ingenious displays. It thus made the artifact management system distinct and orderly while also giving consideration to the safety and ease of retrieval of objects. Such care and attention to methods in dealing with and giving new meaning to the objects reveal new tastes and attributes of this period.

Imitation ancient jade axe pendant (with wooden case and imperial text)
The Ch'ien-lung Emperor appreciated this jade axe pendant so much that an ingenious box in the shape of a book was made for it. Inside is the text "Record of the Ancient Jade Axe Pendant" personally brushed by the Ch'ien-lung Emperor himself. The record states that the object was "promoted" from the third to first rank, making it akin to a "Cinderella" piece in the court collection.

White jade high-stem basin for imperial use with ch'ih-**dragon pattern (with stand and case), Ch'ien-lung reign, Ch'ing dynasty**
A jade cup is given two appearances using a clever design and arrangement of the wooden stand and jade form itself. On the wooden stand, for example, it looks like a small wine cup, but take away the stand and it becomes a tall-stemmed cup.

Collection Seals and Inscriptions on Artifacts

As early as three thousand years ago, many inscriptions were cast or engraved on bronzes. Some of them express the owners' great honor at being able to have such valuable possessions along with the hopes that their pride and joy will be passed down forever to following generations. The seals and inscriptions appearing on works of art allow us to follow the objects as they passed through the hands of owners and collectors through the ages and witness the great joy and honor that these cultural resources brought to subsequent generations.

Jade *pi*-disc (with stand), late Neolithic period
From 1772 until the Ch'ien-lung Emperor retired in 1795, he admired this 4,000-year-old jade *pi*-disc many times. In fact, he had both sides engraved with two of his poems and five of his seals, but do they add or detract from the object?

The Thoughts and Actions of the Emperor

The emperors of the High Ch'ing actively promoted the collection, management, and storage of art works. Not only did they study the objects and have catalogues written, they also established new systems and methods while encouraging discussion and becoming trendsetters. This great cultural project involving vast resources of the state would have a great and far-reaching impact on later generations.

❶

❸

❷

❶"Flying bear with stand, T'ang dynasty" from *Hsi-ch'ing Antiquities*, handwritten edition of the Wen-yüan Pavilion *Complete Library of the Four Treasuries*, Ch'ien-lung reign, Ch'ing dynasty
❷Bronze bear form with inlay of precious materials and silver, Han dynasty
❸Jade bear *tsun* vessel, Ch'ien-lung reign, Ch'ing dynasty
The Ch'ien-lung Emperor had a selection of bronzes from the Ch'ing courts compiled into a catalogue known as *Hsi-ch'ing Antiquities*. Each antiquity included an illustration and a description of its shape, decoration, inscription, dimensions, and state of preservation. This bronze bear is the "Flying bear with stand, T'ang dynasty" mentioned in the catalogue. The Ch'ien-lung Emperor also had this bear used as a model as he ordered craftsmen in Soochow to create a jade version of it.

Splendors of Ch'ing Furniture

The collection of Ch'ing dynasty furniture in the National Palace Museum mainly derives from the imperial residence of Prince Kung (I-hsin), who was the brother of the Hsien-feng Emperor. After the mid-nineteenth century, Prince Kung was in charge of foreign affairs at the Ch'ing court and promoted the study of Western technology in order to improve China's military strength. Despite being a representative of the Western school of thought, he also had a great fondness and taste for traditional Chinese arts.

This group of furniture is done completely in red sandalwood. Although the pieces come from the same source, they were not made as a set, for they includes a mix of styles from the seventeenth to nineteenth centuries as well as both simple and ornate manners. The exhibition is divided into two sections. Based on Ch'ing dynasty court paintings, there is an arrangement for living quarters as well as a studio. The center of attention in the living quarters is the wide and comfortable "lohan" couch accompanied by numerous antiquities to create a visually exciting yet inviting atmosphere. The studio features a regal table as the focal point with a display of various refined antiquities that present a calm and introspective air.

Visually stimulating living quarters

A calm studio

(photo: Chang Chen-shan)

Afternoon Tea at the NPM—San-hsi-t'ang Teahouse

The San-hsi-t'ang teahouse, located on the fourth floor of the National Palace Museum's main building, is named after the "Three Rarities" (San-hsi) studio of the Ch'ien-lung Emperor. These "three rarities" refer to ancient masterpieces of calligraphy treasured by Ch'ien-lung-- Wang Hsi-chih's "Clearing after Snow," Wang Hsien-chih's "Mid-Autumn," and Wang Hsün's "Po-yüan." This modern rendition of the "Three Rarities Studio" now features a trendy interior design fusing various aspects of the traditional Chinese studio, such as stitch-bound books, a depository for Buddhist scriptures, small daybed, and wing room. As an aroma of tea fills the space with a literary atmosphere along with elegant sounds of the zither, it creates an ideal aura of the scholar that imbues the visitor with a brief glimpse into the refined leisure of the past.

The Beauty of Chinese Gardens—Chih-shan Garden

After viewing the treasures of Chinese art and culture in the galleries at the National Palace Museum, why not visit Chih-shan Garden on the eastern side of the museum grounds for a rest? The garden consists of eight scenic spots: the Blue-green Bridge West Pavilion, Listening to Orioles, Brush-washing Pond, Calling Cranes, Pines in Wind Pavilion, Caged Geese, Flowing Cups Winding Stream, and Orchid Pavilion. The lush, green natural scenery features intimate bridges and flowing water, covered corridors, and pavilions that recreate lyrical views as in a Chinese painting, presenting the unlimited beauty of a Chinese garden in a small area.

Visit Info
Open Tuesday to Sunday, 7 a.m. to 7 p.m. Admission is NT$20, but free with any National Palace Museum ticket stub of the same day.

Pleasures of a Lotus Pond–Chih-te Garden

Located on the western fringes of the museum grounds, Chih-te Garden is renowned for its lotus pond. In summer, when the lotuses come into bloom, the pond is filled with tender pink blossoms rising tall from the waters, emitting a fragrance carried by the breeze. The scenery here has enchanted countless photographers and lovers of lotus blossoms. There is also a small path lined by dense banyan trees, the Viewing Clouds Pavilion, and a zigzagging bridge. The garden, though not very big, has always left an unforgettable impression on visitors with its pure and natural beauty.

Visit Info
Unrestricted, free access.

Outdoor Public Art–
Inertia / Exertion

On the east and west wings of the second floor outdoor terraces of the museum main building are several large pieces of stone from Sweden, South Africa, Japan, and Hualien in Taiwan. Different methods of carving have been used to bring out the beauty of each stone in this work by the Japanese sculptor Izumi Masatoshi– "Inertia / Exertion." Izumi Masatoshi specializes in splitting stone to reveal its original texture, presenting the eternal nature of natural stone combined with its polished surfaces. This work forms a natural match with the museum surroundings, offering a sense of presence and openness for a serene and meditative effect.

Visitor Information

Address: 221 Chih-shan Rd., Sec. 2, Taipei 111, TAIWAN, R.O.C.
Tel: +886-2-2882-2021   Fax: +886-2-2882-1440
Website: http://www.npm.gov.tw
Hours: 9 a.m. to 5 p.m. (open daily all year round)
Extended evening hours: Every Saturday 5:00pm~8:30pm (free admission)

Admission:
(1) General: NT$160
(2) Group (ten or more persons): NT$120 each
(3) Local students and military/police: NT$80

Free tours:
(1) Chinese: 9:30 am / 2:30 pm
(2) English: 10:00 am / 3:00 pm
(3) Parent-child guided tour: every Saturday and Sunday 10:00 am / 3:00 pm

Audio tours:
Rental audio tour units in Chinese, English, Japanese, and Korean are available at the audio tour services desk on the first floor of the main building (Exhibition Area I).

Note:
For the convenience and viewing pleasure of others, please observe the following rules:
(1) In the galleries, please refrain from loud conversation, playing, eating and drinking, smoking, or discarding wastepaper on the floor.
(2) Please do not use cell phones in the galleries.
(3) Please wear proper attire when visiting and do not bring pets or toys inside the Museum buildings.
(4) Please also note that no photography or filming whatsoever is permitted in the galleries.

Transportation:
Take the Danshui MRT line to the Shilin station and take bus 255, 304, Red 30, Small 18 or 19 to the National Palace Museum.

＊The original Chinese for this translation is based mostly on contents from National Palace Museum publications compiled by the editorial department.

Selected Bibliography:
Chi Jo-hsin, *Treasures from the Working of Nature: Eight Thousand Years of Antiquities* (Taipei: National Palace Museum, 2006).
Kuo Chi-sheng, *Aesthetics and Form* (Taipei: Linking Publishing, 1982).
Lin Mun-lee, *Splendors of the New National Palace Museum* (Taipei: National Palace Museum, 2007)
The National Palace Museum Monthly of Chinese Art (Taipei: National Palace Museum), vols. 271, 272, 273, 274, 278, 286, 287, 290.
Wang Yao-ting and Fung Ming-chu, *Marvelous Sparks of the Brush: Painting and Calligraphy, Books and Documents* (Taipei: National Palace Museum, 2006).

Meet the New National Palace Museum

Issuer: Lin Chiu-fang
Proofreaders: Teng Shu-Ping, Wang Yao-ting, Fung Ming-chu, Tsai Mei-fen, Yu Peichin, Chen Hui-hsia, Wu Pi-yung, Yu Kuo-ching, Liao Pao-show, Chang Lituan, Shih Ching-fei, Lu Shih-Hao, Tang Pei-ling
Chief editorial consultant: Chang Lin-sheng
Editorial consultant: Chen Jiejin
Chief editor: Lin Chiu-fang
Planning editors: Chang Chin-hsiang, Lin Pei-yu, Chen Meng-ping, Huang Ming-yuan, Chu Hsiang-Yun
Translator and English editor: Donald E. Brix
Art consultant: Chen Yung-mo (ink painter)
Art director: Chiu Liang-cheng
Layout: Sunny Dance Art Planners
Pictures: National Palace Museum
Gallery photos: Huang Li-han
Publisher: Acoustiguide Asia Ltd., Taiwan Branch
Address: 10F, no. 143, Sec. 4, Nanjing E. Rd., Sungshan District, Taipei, Taiwan 105
Tel: +886-2-2713-5355
Fax: +886-2-2717-5403
Website: http://www.acoustiguide.com.tw
Printer: SunRise Art Printing Co., Ltd.

Sixth printing: January 2012
Supervised and licensed by the National Palace Museum
Copyright © 2012 Acoustiguide Asia. All rights reserved.

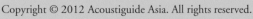